Living and Working
in Other Cultures

Dealing with the Dutch

Living and Working
in Other Cultures

DEALING
WITH THE DUTCH

*The cultural context
of business and work
in the Netherlands
in the early 21st century*

Jacob Vossestein

KIT PUBLISHERS — AMSTERDAM

© 2001 KIT PUBLISHERS – Amsterdam

Cover and design: Henny Scholten, Amsterdam
Cover and Drawings: Franka van der Loo, Amsterdam
Printing: Drukkerij Bariet, Ruinen
Editor: Tony Burrett, Hoorn
ISBN 90 6832 563 9
NUGI 684

The series *Living and Working in Other Cultures* is the continuation of the series *Living and Working in the Tropics:*
Doing business in Africa, C. Ukpabi
Een bestaan als expatriate, F. Quarles van Ufford
Onderhandelen in Zuidoost-Azië, P.R. Voogt
Opgroeien in het buitenland, E. Kunst, M. Simons, F. Öry
Terug naar Nederland, E. Kunst, M. Simons, H. Zorn
Vanuit de partner gezien, I. Groenen

About the author
Jacob Vossestein (1949, Utrecht, the Netherlands) studied human geography and social anthropology and has visited more than 60 countries. As A KIT staff member since 1979 he has developed 'country briefings' for Dutch expatriates-to-be. Since 1988 he has also been responsible for KIT's 'Understanding the Dutch' training programme for foreign managers living in the Netherlands. These are given some 25 times per year for multinational companies such as Shell, Unilever, ABN/Amro bank, Philips, DSM, Quest, and others. As cross-cultural trainer Jacob Vossestein also does introductions to Dutch culture for foreign students and academics, and is involved in the cultural preparations for the international activities of the Dutch armed forces.

CONTENTS

THE NETHERLANDS

- ● City >100.000 inh.
- · Other important towns:
  (not shown in Randstad area)
- Randstad (5 million inh.)
- *Assen* Provincial capital
- Provincial boundaries
- Rivers and canals
- Area less than 1 meter (3,3 ft.)
  above sealevel: without protec-
  tion of dikes or dunes, this
  would be flooded
- Dams and barriers
  (Delta and Zuiderzee projects)

N

Schiermonnikoog
Ameland
Terschelling
WADDENZEE
Delfzijl
GRONINGEN
Groningen
Winschoten
Vlieland
Leeuwarden
Harlingen
Drachten
FRIESLAND
Assen
DRENTHE
Texel
Sneek
Heerenveen
Emmen
Den
Helder
Afsluitdijk
Hoogeveen
Meppel
IJsselmeer
Enkhuizen
Emmeloord
Kampen
NOORD-
Hoorn
Zwolle
Alkmaar
OVERIJSSEL
HOLLAND
FLEVOLAND
Almelo
NORTH SEA
Lelystad
Twente
IJmuiden
Zaandam
Almere
Harderwijk
Deventer
Hengelo
Haarlem Amsterdam
Enschede
Schiphol
Apeldoorn
Veluwe
Zutphen
Hilversum
Amersfoort
GELDERLAND
Leiden
UTRECHT
The Hague
Zoetermeer
Utrecht
Arnhem
Winterswijk
(Den Haag)
Delft
ZUID
Gouda
Wageningen
Betuwe
-6,2 m
Lek
HOLLAND
Rotterdam
Tiel
Nijmegen
Europoort
Waal
Maas
Oss
Dordrecht
GERMANY
's-Hertogenbosch
Oberhausen
NOORD-BRABANT
Duisburg
Roosendaal
Breda
Tilburg
Helmond
Mülheim
ZEELAND
Tholen
Bergen op Zoom
Ruhrgebiet
Walcheren
Eindhoven
Krefeld
Middelburg
Venlo
Düsseldorf
Vlissingen
LIMBURG
Westerschelde
Zeeuws-
Terneuzen
Roermond
Mönchen
Vlaanderen
Gladbach
Antwerp
(Antwerpen)
FLANDERS
Sittard
Gent
Schelde
Heerlen
Kerkrade
BELGIUM
Maastricht
Hills
Aachen
Brussels
(Brussel)
Vaalserberg +312 m
Rhine (Rijn)
IJssel
Maas

ACKNOWLEDGEMENT

I would like to thank my colleagues at KIT who have helped me define the changes going on around us, in particular my fellow-executors on the 'Understanding the Dutch' programmes: Anne Henry, Els de Jong, Marie-Julie Overhaus, Wilfred Ploeg and Juanita Wijnants. Special thanks also to Wouter Swiersta for giving useful comments on the book from the perspective of the younger generation. Needless to say, I am pleased and grateful that KIT Publishers is publishing the revised edition of this book.

And, of course, where would I be without the interesting and often funny observations that the participants of the programmes have shared with me. Their comments contributed much to the success of the first edition and I have no doubt they will do the same for this one.

Finally, I would like to invite readers – foreign or Dutch – to send me their comments. I am always on the lookout for new quotes and for insights, either supporting my ideas or disagreeing with them, and I welcome your reactions. You can reach me by e-mail at *j.vossestein@kit.nl* .

Amsterdam, Spring 2001

GENERAL INTRODUCTION

The subject of this book is the everyday working culture of the Dutch. It is intended for people from other countries who have contacts with the Netherlands through work or business: incoming expatriates, business people coming here for shorter periods, and those who work with the Dutch on a regular basis. For the sake of clarity it should be said that this book is not, and was never meant to be, anything so profound as a manual on Dutch business tycoons, a guide to institutional investors in the Netherlands, a psychoanalysis of the Dutch, or a concise history of the country. What it does try to be is a light-hearted description and fairly accurate explanation of everyday Dutch behaviour, as observed by foreigners encountering the locals in work-related environments, be it just for a few months or for a number of years.

It therefore focuses on the Dutch system of values and norms in the present-day social and economic framework. I set the observations (printed in *italics)* of non-Dutch nationals, who have already had dealings with the Dutch, in the wider context of our culture and society, concentrating on the level of everyday contacts in work and business. I shall tell you what you are likely to encounter here and advise you how to avoid misunderstandings.

Foreigners working with the Dutch seldom experience problems of sloth or inefficiency, inadequate infrastructure or other logistical or 'hardware' problems. Those bringing their families find the general facilities (shops, schools, etc.) are excellent, although it must be said it is neither easy nor cheap to find a suitable place to live. Of course, the initial phase of settling in a foreign country always causes some uneasiness, but once that is over you will have no difficulty with matters such as these.

So what do people complain about? People participating in my programmes keep telling me that it is the underlying values and norms of their Dutch colleagues, counterparts or subordinates that puzzle and sometimes irritate them. Here are a few examples: using different words and phrases they mention the *directness* of the Dutch, the *negative feedback*, the many *rules and regulations* they have to face when settling in, and their Dutch colleagues' strict *separation of work and leisure* time. On a more positive note they are pleased with the *helpfulness* of the Dutch, their *reliability*, the fact that almost *everybody speaks English*, and the readiness to *compromise*.

Norms and values are not static and in recent years Dutch society has been changing quite rapidly. Old religious, ideological and family structures are breaking up, and increasingly, the younger generations have a different, at times even sharply contrasting, view of life and the world than their elders. However, cultural characteristics and 'typical behaviour' don't change overnight. They may reappear in other forms. I have tried to take this into account, on the one hand by sketching the underlying, historical roots of Dutch culture, and on the other by bringing the picture up to date with examples of recent changes that appear to be crucial.

One widespread misunderstanding should be cleared up before we continue. So far, I have used the names 'Holland' and 'the Netherlands' as if they are identical, just two names for the same country. In English, indeed, they are more or less interchangeable, although the more official term 'the Netherlands' is generally used for ceremonial or diplomatic purposes.[1] However, the Dutch themselves call their country 'Nederland' and with just a few exceptions, use the word 'Holland' only to specifically indicate the most important and dominant region of the country: the highly urbanised area in the western provinces, the so-called Randstad (see map). This region is the economic, cultural and political heart of the nation and increasingly functions as one large city of some 7 million people.

Most business encounters with Dutch people take place in the Randstad and you will usually be dealing with 'Hollanders', people who were born in this region or at least live there now. Since this 'Holland proper' exercises a strong overall influence through national institutions and the media this book largely deals with the mentality and behaviour of people in this region. But there are the other areas in the country, and more information on these will be given in chapter 12.

Thus, the following chapters focus on what one might call the 'average' behaviour of the ethnic Dutch majority in business and work. But the Netherlands is fast turning into a multicultural society. Including those from former Dutch colonies (most of whom have Dutch nationality) some two million people from different cultural backgrounds have moved here in recent decades – 15% of the total population. Although many have integrated into Dutch society, the mentality and behaviour of others is not the same as that described in this book. There will be more on the ethnic minorities and immigrant cultures in chapter 11.

Generalisations are inevitable in a book like this. In even the smallest country there are differences in values, views and manners between various groups of the population, between generations, and so on. Some of these issues related to gender and generations are discussed in chapter 10.

As for the business world, another factor is important enough to mention here. The Dutch economy is open and internationally orient- ed and many Dutch business people have been affected by wide exposure to foreign cultures. In their working life, and perhaps in their private life, too, their mentality and behaviour may no longer be 'typically Dutch', but rather reflect a kind of international culture. Business people from other countries frequently find such 'interna- tional' Dutchmen are 'easier' to deal with: *'The Dutch are not all the same. (...) Are they or are they not exposed to an international environment on a more or less daily basis. If they are, then the differences tend to blend away, for instance, their need to leave the office and be home for dinner at six. If they have had more exposure to an international environment, they are more willing to stay until the job is finished.'* (Israel)

But since people with international experience are still in a minori- ty, this book will try to prepare you for more likely situations: dealing with people who behave in a 'typically' Dutch manner. They may be found in smaller companies which are only now beginning to explore cross-border markets, and in larger and/or multinational companies, where not everyone at all levels has had business experience in the outside world.

Dutch mentality and behaviour will be more surprising and strange to people from vastly different cultures such as, say, Nigeria, Malaysia or Brazil, than to people from nearby Germany, Belgium or Britain. But there is a pitfall here for people from our neighbouring countries – just because superficially things in the Netherlands seem to be very much the same as they are at home, they may be fooled into thinking they *are* the same. When they find out there are a million small dif- ferences after all, frustration and culture shock may hit even harder!

But whatever your particular situation, I hope to clarify certain characteristic types of Dutch behaviour you are almost certain to encounter sooner or later.

Throughout the book I will quote observations by people from other countries who are residing in the Netherlands, most of them for reasons of work. I have tried to select quotes which – in my opinion – are not only fairly typical of what people from other countries think of the Dutch, but which also accurately reflect Dutch reality. At the same time I have tried to select quotes that have something 'extra', be it in the phrasing, in the use of metaphors or in the humour .

The quotes were collected by me personally from interviews in Dutch newspapers or magazines, or made to me by participants in the training programmes called 'Understanding the Dutch' at the Royal Tropical Institute (KIT) in Amsterdam.

Some remarks on the revised edition   An old comment on the Netherlands (attributed to the 19th-century German poet Heinrich Heine) says, *'When the world comes to an end, go to Holland because everything happens fifty years later there'*. This may have been true around 1840, but it certainly isn't true in the 21st century. The world is changing, and so is the Netherlands. Nowadays the country is an international forerunner in a wide variety of economic and social fields.

The first edition of this book was written in the winter of 1996 / 1997. Not very long ago, but in some respects it seems a whole century! The term 'Dutch model' or 'polder model', now used frequently in both the Dutch and foreign media, had been coined just in time to be mentioned in the book, while – and this seems quite unbelievable now – the words 'Internet' and 'e-mail' did not appear at all! And although there certainly were references to prosperity it still hadn't become entirely clear that the country was heading for a new wave of increasing wealth.

I recently participated as lecturer in a series of 're-entry' programmes for Dutch people who had lived and worked abroad for some four years. Their residence abroad coincided with the time that had elapsed since the first edition of this book was published. They were quite impressed with the changes that had taken place in their absence. Besides commenting on immediately visible phenomena, such as the fast growing suburbs, heavier traffic on the roads, more non-Dutch faces in the cities, electronic payment ('pinning') facilities in almost every shop, and the importance of e-mail both at work and in social life, they also commented on more abstract changes. They mentioned the increase in wealth and materialism, the influence of free market principles and computerisation in almost every area of life, a decrease in spontaneous human contacts and social cohesion, and even a feeling of aggression in the air.

Clearly these observations also reflect the relaxed lifestyle and warm social contacts of the tropical societies where they had spent the past few years, but that doesn't mean they got it wrong; Holland really *did* change during this period, and it is continuing to do so. When you discuss this with Dutch people who spent these years in the Netherlands – be they people at a party, the proverbial well-informed taxi driver or colleagues at work – you find they have come to the same conclusion.

All in all, a revised edition seems appropriate. It seemed a good idea to include new quotes, fresh observations, by people from other countries who know nothing about Holland as it was before. Continually working with such people and constantly scanning the media, I have collected a wealth of recent quotes and observations and many of these are included in the text.

Another aspect I found relevant to include in this revised edition is the more prominent debate on, and the role of, the ethnic minorities in the Netherlands. The chapter on ethnic variety has been updated to include new developments and debate on this issue.

Not everything changes, though. In my programmes at KIT, foreign managers who arrived here just a few months ago still express their surprise at aspects of Dutch behaviour that I had thought less common today than perhaps they once were. But they DO mention certain things again and again, and when I ask if perhaps it is an older person they are talking about, they deny it: no, fairly young people did so and so, said such and such, reacted in this way or that. Apparently beneath the surface of modernity and market principles, the Dutch are not changing as quickly as they sometimes like to believe - which is why I have decided to keep some quotes from the first edition which I feel are still valid on such subjects.

Certain old-time Dutch characteristics, such as directness, critical attitudes and money-mindedness, still abound. 'New' behaviour may well – consciously or not – be a dissociation from older patterns: 'please let's be different from our parents'. But it often strikes me how during some conflict, when the debate reaches a critical point, the norms and values applied are those firmly rooted in previous periods. Behaviour may have changed, but new norms and values do not appear to have yet crystallised.

It is for this reason that I have included evidence of new phenomena in related parts of the existing chapters. Some parts of the book required complete rewriting, but given the fact that below the surface cultures change very slowly, I still classify apparently 'new' behaviour into the older categories of Dutch culture. At times, my categorising may be debatable, but then, as far as culture is concerned, 'everything is related to everything else'.

So what are these older categories? Well, in years of training foreign business people and other professionals in the field of Dutch culture, I have put together the following list, which forms the basis for the chapters that follow:

Egalitarianism: the idea that people are equal, especially from a moral point of view, and accordingly, the somewhat ambiguous stance the Dutch have towards hierarchy and status;

Directness and critical attitudes: the Dutch are never afraid to voice their many opinions in clear terms;

Pragmatism and *money-mindedness*: a functional approach to life, with an eye open to the financial aspects, but less so for more relationship-oriented matters;

An inclination towards applying fixed *procedures* for almost anything, and yet permissive; tolerant: a land of rules and regulations that still allows everybody to live the way they want to live. Or are they just indifferent?

Internationalism and *openness*: a trading nation that needs to face the world, and does.

Let me begin the description of present-day Dutch mentality by giving you an idea of the changes that have taken place in Dutch society over the last few years.

1. In much the same way the Dutch often use 'England' to refer to the United Kingdom.

Chapter 1

MORE PROSPEROUS THAN EVER BEFORE

'Having one's sheep on dry land'
(old Dutch saying for having made it)

In the spring of 2000, the 'Intelligence Unit' of the British journal *The Economist*, the EIU, declared the Netherlands to be the most attractive market for investments for the period up to 2005 and that the Dutch economy had no evident weaknesses in its business environment.

That same spring, when his company bought the successful Dutch entertainment company Endemol, the managing director of the Spanish media giant Telefónica declared: *'This is certainly not the last thing we'll do here. I like this country very much.'* (Back home he later ran into trouble, but that's another matter).

In 1998, an American investor gave eight reasons why his company had set up business in the Netherlands. He mentioned the stability of the country, the co-operative business climate, the stable currency, Rotterdam as the major gateway to Europe, the availability of a desirable site and of raw materials, the modern infrastructure and the fact that English is widely spoken.

These references are not the only indicators of the present-day success of the Dutch economy. A few more facts: half of the world's multinational companies have a branch office in the Netherlands; Dutch companies are very active on the international financial scene, acquiring large companies in the United States and elsewhere; and small as it is both in area and population, Holland was the world's 8th largest importing and exporting economy in 1999. All governments in the western world know by now what is meant by 'the Dutch model'. The term 'the Singapore of Europe' has been used to describe Holland's economic success.

The Dutch model   The Dutch economic 'miracle' has attracted worldwide attention. Locally known as the *'polder model'*, it indicates a strong economy with permanent high growth and low unemployment, combining internationally competitive wage levels with a good social security system. It started out as an agreement between Dutch employers and trade unions in 1982, when the economy was at a low ebb and unemployment high. The agreement called for changes in the labour market, including a shorter working week, more part-time working, and, in particular, more participation by women (these matters will be discussed elsewhere in this book.)

After a slow start, these changes began to pay off during the 1990s. The Dutch model now also implies a stable social climate, a well-educated and flexible work force, and a favourable tax climate for foreign investors. Seen as a successful model for restructuring rusty welfare states into flexible economies, it was first brought to international attention at the G7 Conference in 1997. President Clinton invited Prime Minister Wim Kok (representing the EU) to explain to the other statesmen present what he termed 'the Dutch model'. Since then, foreign delegations and representatives of the media have visited the Netherlands to study the 'mysterious' harmony between Dutch employers and trade unions – a relationship in which the government keeps a low profile. In Holland itself it is said that cracks are appearing in the model. Some of these will also be mentioned later on in this book.

All this success and wealth has had its effect on Dutch society and on the Dutch way of life. Consumption has risen to unprecedented levels, and it is mostly taken for granted, although there is an undercurrent of disapproval and distrust. Furthermore, the Netherlands has also been deeply affected by the global changes brought about by Internet and e-mail, and the coming of age of a generation that doesn't even remember the times before abundant prosperity, Internet and the CD-ROM.

On an individual level, these young people, especially the well-educated urban professionals, enjoy what they consider to be a far more challenging life than their parents had. They go for the career opportunities the booming economy offers them, for the widely varied choice of entertainment and travel, for the latest electronic devices, for lifestyles based on money and fun. There is a buzz in the air, a flow of energy that is also affecting the older generation.

More and more people are starting up their own company, discovering niches in the market, seeing – and seizing – opportunities. This might be their first working experience or, if they are older, they might be leaving the job they already have. Yet others choose to combine a part-time job with a small private enterprise. Since many organisations also prefer to hire people on a project basis rather than on a full contract, there are many opportunities to make your dreams come true.

Due to this growth and flexibility, for most people consumption has risen to hitherto unknown levels and for several years now consumer trust in the economy has been – and is – at an almost constant high. As a result, the average debt of Dutch households, although still fairly low in comparison to other European countries, is rising. Before continuing, I would like to list some random new phenomena which have appeared in the Netherlands during the last few years (these have all been culled from the Dutch media).

The buoyant labour market   Unemployment has been below 3% already for some time now. Many organisations cannot find enough employees. Shops, supermarkets, cafés and restaurants, schools, hospitals and dental clinics, trucking and construction companies, even the police and the army are having problems finding qualified, or even semi-qualified, people. As a result vacancies are being filled by new labour immigrants – Indian ITC experts, nurses from the Philippines and from South Africa, teachers and construction workers from Germany.

• Economic growth has been around 4% for several years now. This is one of the highest in Europe, and prospects remain good.

• The Dutch parliament is discussing how to handle large budget *surpluses* rather than deficits.

• Job-hopping is on the increase, with well-educated younger people, in particular, preferring high payments and greater risk to permanent jobs and security.

• More competition and financial inequality. There is a growing difference between top salaries and those at the bottom of the labour market. The days when the Netherlands had one of the most equal distributions of income in the world are over.

• After evening closing time for shops was relaxed some years ago, in city centres many shops are now also open on Sundays;

• For the first time in history more Dutch people now *own* their house than *rent* it. But with lots of money about and low interest rates the housing market is overheated – to the despair of many natives as well as expatriates!

• Partly financed by the resulting increased value of their property, many people now own shares and actively play the stock market.

• Computers, Internet, e-mail and mobile phones have become normal attributes, both at work and in private households.

• Obesity is increasing among all age groups and is beginning to become a problem. Parents and medical authorities are worried that some 10% of Dutch children are seriously overweight.

• Zapping as a lifestyle. More and more people are shopping around to satisfy their momentary needs, resulting in decreasing loyalty to political parties, broadcasting organisations, newspapers, volunteer organisations, etc.

• The rise of new professions such as 'personal shoppers', dog-walkers, food caterers, etc.

• Car ownership is higher than ever before. With 6.5 million cars plus some 500.000 other vehicles, the density of over 200 vehicles per km^2, or 500 per sq.mi., is the highest in the world, leading to constant traffic jams. These now also occur in less-densely-populated provinces, at weekends and late at night.

Concerns *'The trees seem to be growing into heaven'*, is a Dutch saying used to indicate a certain distrust of a seemingly positive condition. And indeed, not everything is to everybody's liking in our rich, pluriform society. In January 2000, research[2] was published on the issues which Dutch people are concerned about. The ten problems most mentioned were: rising crime (a concern to 92% of those interviewed), the state of nature and the environment (72%), the position of people on minimum income (71%), AIDS, unemployment, the number of people on WAO benefit (more on this in chapter 7), traffic jams, asylum seekers (see chapter 11), rising house prices, and the national debt.

On a more philosophical level, a number of intellectuals and representatives of the churches have expressed dismay about the new consumerism, increasing selfishness and anti-social behaviour. In her radio talks at Christmas Queen Beatrix regularly warns against outright materialism and egoism, against the impersonality of modern society and the erosion of traditional norms and values. Many people agree. They worry about the increase in random violence, and react with horror when they read about mafia killings, even though these rarely affect ordinary people's lives.

It isn't just the older generations who are irritated by loud mobile phone conversations on public transport, by aggressive driving in city streets and on motorways[3], and other manifestations of lack of consideration for others. And not only people from traditional Calvinistic backgrounds have mixed feelings about the tendency in society towards 'sheer fun', where getting into the *Guinness Book of Records* for some silly achievement seems more important than keeping an eye on ageing neighbours.

All around them people see the old pastoral landscapes disappearing and being replaced by more and more highways, 'science parks' and new suburbs. Space might well be the scarcest commodity in this country! A new organisation is pleading – explicitly on non-racist grounds – for the return to a population of just 10 million people.

When one lives in Holland one has to come to terms with the paradox of the good luck and comfort of living in a prosperous and peaceful country, and the concerns that there are less fortunate aspects for society as a whole and many individuals in it. *'I think the Dutch should watch out what all this wealth may do to them. Being rich changes people, it makes them hard and selfish.'* (Ethiopia)

Let me give you a comment by Sylvain Ephimenco, an Algerian-French author who wrote several rather critical books on Dutch society. In an interview[4] he said: *'You know, everything I have written about Holland since let's say the end of the 1980s should be taken with a grain of salt. So much has changed. It is striking and fascinating at the same time to see how the old Calvinism has been shaken off. There are new opportunities, there is more openness. There is a kind of mutation taking place in the Dutch soul: the stiffness, the strictness, perhaps also there is less hypocrisy: people now dare to be open in what they do, like buying shares. That's good, there is more air, but at the same time, with all the consumerism, the pendulum also swings the other way. (…) But what is so amazing is the great leap forward – or whatever you want to call it – has proved to be so much wider than elsewhere. It goes from one extreme to the other.'* The speed of change in Dutch society, was also brought up by Mrs. Maria Bogyay, a Hungarian living in Holland, who writes on Dutch-Hungarian relations.[5] She told me: *'Recent developments and attitudes seem to contradict everything I always felt to be 'typical' about the Dutch'.*

Uniquely Dutch?   Several of the changes, of course, are not a uniquely Dutch phenomenon, but in a crowded country with little chance to get away from it all, the exposure to such things may be more intense than elsewhere. Small wonder, perhaps, that alongside the vast crowds of successful people and those who live life to the full, there are people who turn their back on society, people with psychological troubles, people with severe depression, people who simply cannot cope. Others turn to crime or violence to vent their perceived feelings of deprivation or exclusion.

Both politicians and the media in Dutch society pay attention to all this, with quite a lot of concern.

Some speak of a 'fragmentation' or even an 'atomisation' of society, indicating increased individualism. Others use the older term *twee-deling* (pron. _tway-dayling_, meaning duality, dualism), a 'split' between the true participants in the booming economy and those left out, or left behind. Given the conditions of Dutch society, this is not quite the same as 'winners' and 'losers', although, with its psychological impli-cations, it comes close. Examples of groups left behind – perhaps financially but more so regarding opportunities in society – are single mothers, old people without children living solely on state old-age benefit, people with mental problems, and the homeless. It is estimated that taken together such groups comprise between 10 and 20% of the population.[6] They share a certain isolation, a lack of con-tacts or networks, a sad feeling they have been left to themselves without much real support. The fact that in many countries people in similar positions are far worse off financially, if recognised at all, doesn't help them very much.

Sometimes the term *tweedeling* is also used in relation to those who – for whatever reasons – are unable to participate in the buzzing digital world of information and education that is all around them.

In yet another context, *tweedeling* may refer to the position of ethnic groups in Holland, at least to certain categories among them. In chapter 11 we will explore these developments.

More American? Now readers from other European countries and certainly from North America may think this isn't so very different from their own country. But not all readers come from the western world, and moreover, through my work I have noticed that even in quite a few countries of Western Europe such changes seem to hap-pen at a slower pace than here in Holland.

Like most Europeans, the Dutch have mixed feelings about the United States, but quite a few Dutch people would agree that the recent changes could be collectively described as a 'more American' lifestyle. Already for some decades the Dutch tend – jokingly – to see their country as a candidate for becoming the 51st state of the USA, and this feeling has only grown with the changes described above.

Americans themselves, however, apparently feel differently. In an interview with a Dutch newspaper, a top American consultant was asked to comment on the fact that the Netherlands sees itself as 'the most American country in Europe'. All he said was: *'Hmmm? Interesting....'*, adding immediately that so does the UK. On one of my courses, an American expatriate commented, mostly referring to family life and shopping facilities in the Netherlands: *'At first, living in Holland felt like going back in time twenty years, but now after some time we like it a lot.'*

Most Dutch people would probably react to this with a mixture of disbelief and curiosity, as I did, since being called 'old-fashioned' isn't really considered a compliment. (On second thoughts, following American news as closely as do the Dutch media, perhaps it isn't all that bad…)

Despite the worries outlined above – which are not immediately visible to newcomers – to most other foreigners Dutch society definitely comes across as not only modern, liberal, open and flexible, but also as humane and relaxed. When I described Dutch work ethics and regulations to an American interviewer, she reacted: *'That's exactly why I chose to live here, in spite of all the bureaucracy it cost me to legally do so!'*

Yet it's true; there are a lot of things in Holland that are not at all American, not even like the America of the 1980s. Americans themselves mention the ongoing strong 'family orientation' in most of Dutch society, the near-taboo on discussing one' s religion in public, the uncensored nudity and sex on television , the wide acceptance of homosexual relationships and the relative safety on the streets even after dark.

So the country is changing along with the rest of the world, perhaps faster, but in its own way. Even the basic tenets of Dutch society are no longer quite the way they were: after centuries of pushing back the water, some land is now being given back to the old enemy. In the field of religion the secularisation process has gone so far that even most 'native Dutch' children hardly know the significance of Christian holidays such as Easter and Pentecost. With the waning of religion and the growing influence of the market economy, the old differences between the North and the South seem to be fading more and more. There is even a debate regarding the role of the monarch, which, according to some politicians, should be limited.

In another field, although foreigners still comment with some amazement on the amounts of bread and milk the Dutch consume, local producers see only decreasing markets for these products, while – at least in the cities – vendors of ricotta, kwikwi, piri-piri, starfruit or brownies no longer have to explain their products to their cus-tomers. Even the national reputation for speaking several languages fluently needs some revision now that the Dutch only want to learn to speak English and no longer appear to be interested in German and French. The old Calvinistic virtues of thrift and sobriety are hard to find these days, with people consuming like never before and spending their money on luxurious goods and lifestyles.

Yet quite a bit of the old remains – if not always in visible behaviour, then at least in the underlying values and the comments people make if others show them. In other words: the value system hasn't yet changed altogether. This is certainly the case among the vast majority of people who do NOT work in the ITC sector, who do NOT work abroad, who do NOT fly back and forth to New York or Singapore all the time. For visiting business people and expatriates settling in the Netherlands – and they are the target group of this book – such less 'globalised' people make up a large portion of the people they encounter at work and in their private lives. So let's start exploring the characteristics of the majority of the Dutch, and the society they created.

1. 'Polder' is the Dutch word for reclaimed land, made out of water or swampland, through strict water-control. Low and grassy, mostly used for keeping cows, polder land makes up a large part of the Netherlands.
2. By Bureau Lagendijk, Apeldoorn.
3. In 2000, the Dutch were found to be the second most aggressive drivers in Europe, after the British.
4. Sylvain Ephimenco in *VPRO gids*, Sept. 16, 2000.
5. *Hongaars-Nederlandse bespiegelingen*, by Maria Bogyay (Lemma, Utrecht 1997).
6. In December 2000, the number of truly poor people in Dutch society was said to have gone down by several percents in just a few years.

Chapter 2

ON IMAGES AND STEREOTYPES

'Ah, you're from Holland? Such a nice little country,
with flowers everywhere. Pity it always rains there.'
(French lady talking to the author
on a train from Paris to Nice)

'The Netherlands has a good reputation among Africans. My friends in other EU-countries like to come here. It's a kind of safe haven. You don't notice too much discrimination here, but if I go to France the police pick me out immediately.' (Nigerian asylum seeker in a newspaper interview)

Almost everyone has preconceived ideas, frequently generated by the media, of other countries and the people who come from them. Even the remotest country inspires some mental picture, however vague or stereotyped, of what it might be like. Of course, stereotypes are not wholly representative, but neither are they wholly unrepresentative. They usually reflect certain characteristics, maybe out of context or outdated, or stripped of their real meaning and function, but characteristics nonetheless. Yet the stereotype is what most people start from, it colours their expectations and their initial perceptions. But particularly when we work among or with the people to whom the stereotype refers we gradually learn how valid the generalisations, the contexts, the nuances really are. The same, of course, applies to the stereotypes about Holland and the Dutch.

The Netherlands is not exactly a remote country, being in the heart of Europe, and it features regularly in the international media. This means that different people have different images of our country, some more accurate than others, some suggested by Dutch institutions, some definitely not. The images prevalent abroad differ widely. They depend on the observer's national origins because the way a person perceives a foreign country always involves that person's own cultural background.

This can be seen in virtually all the quotations reproduced in this book, which besides commenting on the Dutch usually also reveal something of the observers' own frame of reference. For example, the French lady's comment above says something of France too – its size, its climate and the apparent lack of flowers in her hometown. The Nigerian compares his experiences in France with his friends' experiences in Holland. Opinions like these often reflect the observer's social position and the sources from which (s)he acquired the information. It makes quite a difference whether one reads (certain) newspapers, or has worked with Dutch people, or made several short business visits to the Netherlands, or had contact in any other way.

Be that as it may, let us try and make an inventory of the most important images of Holland that surface in foreign publications and opinion. We will come to the economic image later, but let's first briefly look at some others. Some of these are major factors in attracting incoming expatriates, others are not:

The sturdy image: (popular in geography books) a flat, wet country, most of it lying below sea level. A place where it never stops raining and which would surely be flooded if it were not for the windmills, the famous Delta Works and little Hans Brinker sticking his finger in the dyke. In 1995 this image was reinforced by international media coverage when the great rivers in the centre of the country threatened to burst their banks and entire towns and villages and hundreds of farms were evacuated.

The tourist image: a largely agrarian idyll. Charming Queen Beatrix ruling an innocent little country, the inhabitants of which wear wooden shoes and ride bicycles and peacefully produce milk and cheese, flowers and flower bulbs. And those who don't live in windmills live in old, quaintly-gabled houses beside canals.

The cultural image: a small country with a great tradition in the arts. Famous painters past and present, their works on display in wonderful museums; also renowned for its world-famous symphony orchestras and ballet companies and as a good place for avant-garde theatre. Nowadays it is also famous as a source of great literature, which the outside world reads in translation.

The permissive, lenient image: (emphasised – from rather different angles – by foreign journalists and young travellers, but sometimes a source of concern to foreign investors) a place where apparently anything goes. Although most of the journalists and the travellers usually hang around in downtown Amsterdam, they depict all of the Netherlands as a (far too) liberal society, where specialised shops sell legal drugs and pornography to people indulging in nudity. A nation that finds it perfectly normal for gay couples (married in the Town Hall, of course) to obtain children by artificial insemination, and where people are helped to die by itinerant doctors legally practising euthanasia. Luckily for Holland, investors soon discover that much of this image is half-true at best, and that there is a lot more to Dutch society than this.

The humane image: linked to the permissive image, but from yet another perspective, is the idea held by immigrants and political refugees coming into Europe, of the Netherlands as a comfortable 'safe haven'. Judging from the number of people arriving the word has gone round that this is a country with wide-ranging political and religious freedom, where authorities are perhaps more strict than they used to be but still 'humane', and where sooner or later work – or at least social benefits – will be available.

On the global scene, the Netherlands is also seen as a country that takes seriously its international obligations in providing development assistance. It not only finances international peace missions but also takes part in them, and presents initiatives in environmental and other global issues etc.

The image of being blunt and opinionated: (discussed among expatriates and hinted at in diplomatic circles) a tiny country with a big mouth, wanting to appear larger than it is, its people tactlessly expressing their views on other people's and other nations' affairs.

The sporting image: a nation of excellent football teams. Well, traditionally, that is; they haven't won very much recently. Unfortunately, hooligans violently expressing anti-German sentiments accompany the teams when they play against German opposition. The Dutch also have a good reputation in other sports – ice-skating, swimming, tennis, hockey, and even darts – although they are not always aware of this. Dutch national hockey teams are among the best in the world, but club hockey is lucky to receive a few minutes television coverage on Sunday evenings.

The tight-with-money image: in neighbouring countries the Dutch are seen as money-minded people whose greatest pleasure is extracting every last guilder out of any transaction. Many are convinced that when they go on holiday elsewhere in Europe the Dutch load up their caravans with food from their supermarket rather than spend money in local restaurants. As a result, all the way down to the shores of the Mediterranean street vendors comment (in Dutch!) on Dutch shoppers with the slogan 'kijken, kijken, niet kopen': looking, looking, not buying. Which brings us to the final image.

The economic image: even aside from the 'polder model', the Dutch economy is taken very seriously. Small as it is, the Netherlands is the world's eighth largest trading nation. With Rotterdam being the world's busiest harbour and Schiphol a major airport, the Netherlands promotes itself as 'the Gateway to Europe'. Moreover, it is home to multinational companies such as Royal Dutch Shell, Unilever, Philips, Heineken, KLM, Akzo-Nobel, Ahold and DSM, and financial institutions such as ABN/Amro, Aegon and ING. Based in a small but very wealthy home market, all these companies – and others – are globally active. Certainly doing more than 'just looking', they expand into international markets, acquiring majority shareholdings (often at a very favourable price) or even outright ownership of foreign companies. Perhaps slightly less known but equally impressive are Holland's dairy industry, which supplies half the world with cheese and milk powder, and, less traditionally, Endemol, an entertainment factory producing programmes for TV stations throughout the western world.

All these images may be over-generalised and over-simplified, but many Dutch people will recognise them. Sometimes they agree with them, although they will probably not let them pass without comment (which, of course, fits in nicely with their image of always knowing better than everyone else).

The wide range of the stereotypes reflects a pluriform society, which accommodates a broad variety of life-styles and views within a very small country. When we condense them, an image emerges of a country that does not avoid challenges but is willing to try solutions that may be out of the ordinary.

This sounds rather fascinating and provocative, and it could easily evoke the idea that the Netherlands is a land of non-conformists. There certainly are such people around, and Dutch television happily presents them to an eager audience. Yet most people who come from other countries see the Netherlands in a quite different light: they see a highly organised society of great regularity, a country where public transport runs on time[1], where rules written and unwritten are respected, where, in spite of all the permissiveness, most people seem to follow a set pattern of daily activities. As an illustration, a Spanish lady working in Holland exclaimed: *'Sometimes I wonder if the Dutch have blood in their veins, or milk!*

This picture is quite contrary to the one painted earlier: conformity rather than unconventionality, boring rather than fascinating. The Spanish lady's comment reveals something of the despair someone from a more emotional, warm-blooded culture may experience here.

And yet there *are* all those sex shops and coffee shops selling soft drugs, there *are* those social experiments, ground-breaking laws and daring solutions, and there are all those stubborn Dutch who will insist on going their own way, despite convention. More paradoxes, in other words.

1. This is a foreign compliment that amazes Dutch people. Not familiar with other countries' public transport, they complain that trains and buses are always late, they never run when you need them and – of course – they are too expensive. In defence of this Dutch view, it must be said that foreigners usually base their positive opinion on experiences in the well-serviced Randstad area.

Chapter 3

HIERARCHY,
AND THE DUTCH PROBLEM WITH IT

'Geen kapsones!'
(Dutch slang expression, rebuking perceived 'airs', arrogance)

As a result of the Balkan wars and massive migration, terms like 'nation', 'culture', 'ethnicity' and 'identity' are being heard all over Europe. As the European Union discusses extending membership to other countries, even nations with a fairly homogeneous population are becoming somewhat insecure about their identity: who are we, what is our essential nature, what do we want to preserve in a united Europe? This is also true of the Dutch, although they have been protagonists of European co-operation since 1945 – and not just because their trading economy thrives on open borders. But now that European unification is really dawning, doubts are beginning to set in. The euro is about to replace the guilder, and 'Brussels' already has at least an equally important role in Dutch legislation as The Hague. But where will it all lead? Will the cultural and social achievements of smaller countries such as Holland be safeguarded? Can the Dutch language, identity and institutions survive in the long run? What about the flag and the national anthem? And should we accept being a country of immigration or not?

In an interview preceding his state visit of February 2000, the French president, Jacques Chirac, compared France and the Netherlands. After flattering the Dutch with Latin charm by pointing out their country's strength as an economic, diplomatic and even military power, he pointed out: *'France and the Netherlands have a lot in common (...) They are two nations with a distinct character. (...) Ideas like independence, national grandeur and the respect for people and human rights are just as important to the French as to the Dutch. The French respect for identity and independence can be seen equally strongly among the Dutch.'*

This may make the Dutch feel good, but it is not the general image they hold of themselves. In fact, they tend to take these aspects for granted and try to look a little deeper into their own souls. In discussions on the questions as to what exactly Dutch identity is and what sets the Dutch apart from other nations, various journalists and philosophers came to the conclusion that at the heart of Dutch culture lies 'egalitarianism', a sense of everyone being equal from a *moral* point of view. Although there are some financial aspects to it, far more important is the underlying ethical principle that everyone should have the same opportunities and that no matter what people's position in society, high or low, they should be treated equally and with fairness. The major condition is – low profile behaviour. If people do indeed occupy a high place in society they shouldn't openly pride themselves on it, while those in more lowly positions have the right to speak up, too.

In everyday reality the egalitarianism issue is quite complex, and it has a number of subtle effects, both in general Dutch society and in the business world. The overall effect is that the Dutch have difficulty in dealing with hierarchy, always trying to maintain a balance between being aware of the hierarchical aspects of a relationship and not wanting to make that awareness too obvious.

I first want to explore these general effects: attitudes towards hierarchy and excellence, the class-orientation of Dutch society, and aspects of status. This is the context, explaining much of the everyday behaviour in work and business, on which we then focus in more detail in the next chapter.

It is not easy, especially for foreigners, to immediately see egalitarianism as an essential value. It lies somewhat hidden in Dutch behaviour and institutions, and it may be some time before foreigners understand its scope. What they do notice from the start is a certain lack of decorum, the casual way in which many Dutch people deal with hierarchy and status , the approachability of authorities, and the do-it-yourself aspect of society. They sense, for instance, a lack of appreciation for outstanding performances, or a certain uniformity in (modern) Dutch housing, or a surprising degree of workers' participation in companies.

More examples will be given later, but all these things can only be explained by taking into account Dutch egalitarianism. It is deeply rooted in history and, according to some observers, even in the flat landscape. It has quite a few consequences for people's everyday behaviour, both in and outside the business world. Even conduct apparently quite contradictory to egalitarianism is often, consciously or not, nothing but a dissociation from this core-value. This is how one foreigner perceived it: *'If anyone here sticks out from the crowd, his head is chopped off. There is always criticism. They always tear people down, good performance is played down. Everyone must be the same, there shouldn't be anyone brilliant.'* (Argentine) And a young Dutch business-man with international work experience added: *'All this egalitarianism irritates me. We don't allow heroes or prominent people. We daren't be proud without inhibitions. Except on the odd occasion when we become world champions in skating or football.'*

'Just act normal, that's strange enough' In fact this much-used Dutch expression says it all. It is informally used as an ironic comment when someone's behaviour or opinions are perceived as being out of the ordinary or overdone. It is a call for conventionality; blend in with everybody else, conform, don't stick out. Looking at all the wealth around them, foreigners sometimes don't believe me: *'Come on, this may have been true twenty years ago, but NOW!? There are seven Jaguars parked in the street where we live! OK, it's a well-to-do area, but still!'* (USA). I then try to explain that 'egalitarianism' is not directly related to people's wealth or possessions, but rather to their attitu-des. It is not a kind of communism but a moral state of mind. One may drive a Jaguar, but when this leads to haughty behaviour, or is percei-ved to do so, then it will be criticised (as we will see below ...).

This may come as a surprise in a country that also has a reputation for permissiveness. On closer inspection one might realise that the call for equality, for conformity, relates not so much to the behaviour or opinion itself, but to the moral stance that people might attach to it. They may be very special indeed but that should not make them feel or behave as if they are superior to others. The message is: be or do whatever you want, but don't boast of it, don't expect privileges, or more respect than anyone else. Dutch advertisements on radio and TV use actors playing cocky, elite people with affected voices in order to get some easy laughs.

Common people are the accepted norm, the elite can be mocked. Neither material extravagancies nor high profile behaviour are appre-ciated. On the other hand, any individual that is, or can make others believe he is, a victim of injustice, an underdog, can certainly count on a degree of support, either from other individuals or from a political party or action group. One might see Dutch society as an upside-down pyramid – certainly in the public sector the large majority of ordinary people (being middle class) are the overall norm, the elite merely facilitate them in exchange for silent acceptance of their prominent position. A few examples: for decades virtually all houses built in cities were of the size and taste of 'average' middle and lower class families. The tax system is meant as a kind of 'levelling device', skimming the rich, uplifting the underprivileged, bringing everyone to the middle ground. Business tycoons, politicians or intellectual 'big shots' get far less public attention than people representing common taste: football players, TV artists and presenters. They may be seen as riding a bike, having a simple lunch, camping out or walking along the beach, just as 'normal' as anyone else. In the business world this attitude may be less prevalent, but it is not completely absent. The public impression of being a good family man and just an average consumer helps to make these big shots acceptable.

In most countries, one has a far easier life when high up in society than when one belongs to the lower levels. The high-ups are given – or take – all the chances, they get the privileges, they make the rules. In the Netherlands the myth that the opposite is true is upheld. In exchange for the social harmony that keeps their privileges silently intact, the elite lies low. Anyone with authority or with exceptional talents should make it clear through his/her behaviour, between the lines so to speak, that although (s)he may have power, money or prestige, (s)he is nonetheless modest, approachable and democratic. Australians recognise their *'the tall-poppy syndrome'* in this. But Americans, especially, perceive it as a lack of competitiveness, suspecting that this attitude leads to mediocrity. Observers from quite different cultural backgrounds think otherwise, however: *'Everybody here is competitive'* (Russian businessman working in Holland, speaking to young Russian managers being trained in Holland), while another Argentinean, an academic researcher, remarks: *'Since I came here several years ago, I have learned a lot and met many nice people, but you have to fight here to achieve something. You have to prove yourself again and again.'*

Both points of view are correct, in a way. The Russian and the second Argentinean are right because the Dutch economy, or the sports world or even academia, can hardly be called non-competitive. But the Australian and the Americans have a point too: on a smaller scale, between individual people, competition is not greatly appreciated. Whether among schoolchildren, university students, co-workers in a company or members of a sports club, the feeling is that it is fine to try and be the best, but don't overdo it, a modest victory is usually good enough and you certainly shouldn't compete at the expense of weaker players or colleagues.[1] Perhaps this observation by a young German studying in Amsterdam may serve as a good illustration: *'Dutch students have different attitudes towards grades* (than Germans). *The Dutch are content with a mere 5.6* (in Holland, with a 0 to 10 grading system in education, that is the exact minimum to pass an exam, JV). *Once I witnessed a guy who answered just six out of ten questions at an exam and then left. He explained to me: 'I got these six questions all right, why should I bother doing the rest?'*

Another example might be the now infamous case of a brilliant high school student who wanted to study medicine. At Dutch universities medicine is a subject for which there are more applicants than places, so a kind of lottery system is employed. This brilliant girl had to draw a number like anyone else. For three consecutive years she struck out. The case received much media attention and was even discussed in parliament. But in the end no exception was made and the girl went to Belgium to study.

This certainly seems to prove the American point of 'reinforcing mediocrity', and even among the Dutch it caused disapproval, but in the end the core value of egalitarianism prevailed, as well as 'the same rules for everyone' principle, see chapter 7. (For a better perspective of the decision, it should be added that studying at Dutch universities is subsidised and, compared to American universities, not very expensive. Moreover, a fairly wide government scholarship programme helps anyone to study academically. Yet, most Dutch students complain about both these things, not realising how lucky they are...)

Academic titles: In Dutch society the use of academic titles is mostly limited to the functional working environment and then in writing only, on business cards and letters. Using them in private life or in speech does occasionally occur, but most people find this boastful rather than respectable. Another observation by the German student quoted above: *'I find the teachers here much more approachable than those in Germany. You have to address the latter with 'Herr Professor', but in Holland that isn't so. Here you can just go for a beer with your teacher.'*

If titles are not backed up by reality – as happens in some countries – their use is a social disgrace, as one well-known Dutchman found out. He decided to disappear abroad to really get the degree. When he came back to Holland years later he started a consultancy firm for people whose reputations had been damaged. Then, when it was found out he still didn't have a degree, his name became a metaphor.

Competition   The issue of competition deserves further attention. Until recently there were quite a few price agreements or sometimes even outright monopolies within the Dutch economy. Besides the obvious economic benefits for the companies involved, people in the same industry in a small country tend to know each other. As long ago as 1968, a union leader called Mertens brought to public attention the network of some 200 'old' families, all knowing each other personally, and holding key positions in the economy, in politics and other high places. You may see it as a Dutch version of the British 'old boy network' or the Finnish 'sauna society'. Indeed there are family names that keep cropping up in various influential fields.

With increased social mobility, these days the so-called 'Mertens 200' is probably a larger group, but perhaps less of a solid block. Yet the basic condition still exists. Seeing each other on all kinds of social occasions, serving on various boards, meeting in business clubs and theatres, and job-rotating between different companies and organisations, too much competitiveness was very much frowned upon by these people. There was an unspoken agreement on harmonious live-and-let-live arrangements. Cartels and other non-competitive co-operation resulted.

Even in the current more market-oriented climate, the government organisation set up to break open such strongholds (the NMa, or Dutch competition authority), has still not finished its job. On the other hand, the present government has privatised various former state companies in the field of public utilities: energy, water, transport and telecommunication. Now there is increasing criticism that this has gone too far, especially because these new companies may have to face *national* competition but still have *regional* monopolies, be it for a restricted period. The privatising of the energy companies has not brought down consumer prices so far, while in the summer 2000 auction of UMTS-frequencies for mobile phones, the major Dutch telecom-companies were also found to be quietly co-operating and keeping outsiders out. This led to far lower revenues for the state than in neighbouring countries. When it was found that Dutch gasoline prices were the highest in the EU (even before taxation), suspicions immediately rose… On a slightly more modest level, Dutch bicycle makers have also been accused of silent price fixing.

Taxi wars   A good example of Dutch resistance to competition is the 'taxi war' in Amsterdam. TCA, an organisation of semi-independent taxi drivers, had had a monopoly for many years. In the past, drivers had to buy much-sought after taxi permits, for which a kind of black market had sprung up. With market liberalisation these permits became far easier and cheaper to obtain, leading the TCA drivers to complain of injustice and inequality. In 2000, after the city refused compensation, they actively resisted the entry of other taxi companies into the market. First there was only verbal abuse, but as no compromise was reached some new drivers were beaten up by their older 'colleagues', and their cars damaged. Various attempts at reaching an agreement, proposing a kind of geographical division of the city, were unsuccessful. At the moment of writing no final solution is in sight.

Personal attitudes   Although top class performers in the fields of the arts, sport and business are certainly applauded in Holland, people think they should remain 'human' and accessible to everyone. They should behave with some modesty, appreciate their fellow competitors and share their glory with others. Anyone lending assistance or support should participate in their victory, be mentioned by name, hauled up onto the rostrum with the winner. If this doesn't happen terms like 'swaggering' and 'arrogance' soon crop up.

The basic idea of the equality issue is that everyone merely uses the talents they happen to have. To have them is good fortune, nothing more. Until not so long ago, such talents were considered to be God-given. It was considered one's duty to use them for the benefit of all. Thus very talented people should be grateful rather than expect applause. (Indicative of this attitude, perhaps is the relative absence in most Dutch cities of monuments to national heroes and other figures. The few that can be found were usually put up long after the hero had died.)

Nowadays, with secularisation, being talented is not considered to be God-given, but a natural coincidence, a fortunate DNA structure, the result of good education, anything except strictly personal excellence. To me, this is proof of the not-so-individualistic attitude of the Dutch, a touch of collectivism (see chapter 10). You may be good but remember that you owe it to others, divine or human. Never forget the context, the external factors so to speak, that helped to make you who you are, and find a way to pay your dues. Later we will see how this works out in practice, in social responsibility, in charity work and in contributing to society by (more or less) honestly and obediently paying one's taxes.

High working morals   Clearly in Dutch culture no one is essentially any better than anyone else. Success should not go to one's head. An old rhyme, still quoted, can be translated as: 'Those who don't appreciate the small, don't deserve the large'. So those with talent should deploy it for the benefit of all, not just for themselves. This indicates, generally speaking, that the Dutch have high working morals. Being useful, being busy, not idling, is considered a virtue. If you happen to be very talented naturally you will reap the benefits, but you should keep quiet about it and just do your duty. Be equal, after all!

In private life, too, hanging around, not doing anything constructive, is usually frowned upon, unless it is 'deserved' relaxation after some kind of fruitful activity. One can be almost sure that the relaxed people one observes in street-cafés on sunny afternoons have just finished being 'useful' or are about to be so again soon.

The other day, an American journalist asked me: *'Are foreigners who assume the Dutch are lazy right?'* I am aware that foreigners perceive this country as a relaxed place (see chapter 8), but in reply I told her to never use this L-word to a Dutch audience, because they themselves are convinced they work very hard. Many Dutch people are aware that the Netherlands has one of the highest productivity figures per hour worked, and many were raised by parents saying things like 'Hard work never killed anybody'.

No, the Dutch aren't lazy. What may lead foreigners to think so is that most Dutch people work relatively few hours per week and enjoy long holidays - but this shouldn't be confused with laziness, it is seen as a reward for the otherwise busy lives they lead. In fact, when asked how you are doing, it's something of a status thing to reply *'druk, druk, druk'*, that is: busy, busy, busy. Significantly, the word also means 'pressure'.

Although this is the image the Dutch have of themselves many foreigners working here see things differently: *'After hearing about all these Dutch successes, one expects the Dutch to work really hard. But in reality they don't, they all run home at five and even during work hours, they're not particularly effective. So in my view they just organise the work better. They're very involved in the company, that's probably where the results come from.'* (Peru) And: *'They talk a lot, don't work very hard, but are friendly.'* (Ireland)

It should probably be admitted that the Dutch, although they may think differently, don't work much harder than other people. A fairly small segment of the population does work very hard, especially at top levels, but for the rest Holland's present wealth may largely be the result of the country catching up with other western nations in the context of a favourable world economy. More flexibility in the labour market and in the housing sector, the fairly sharp rise in population largely due to immigration, the profits from both the increase in house prices and the sharp rises on the stock market, and the integration into the labour market of hitherto 'in-actives' such as women, have all played a role.

Labour satisfaction   In a representative survey of labour satisfaction, held[2] in six west-European countries in 2000, 80% of the Dutch interviewees declared they liked going to work, second only to the Germans who scored 86%, and way ahead of the Spanish with 57%. Just 23% of the Dutch said that money was their sole reason for working. All others gave additional reasons like contacts with colleagues, a sense of fulfilment etc. For more on work incentives, see chapter 6.

So use your talents, no matter what they are. The successful and famous should humbly accept the privileges they are granted. They should not spend their fortune on selfish pleasures but allow others to share in it to at least some degree. Let me give a recent example; nothing special in many countries, but here it caused political upheaval and public discussion, that lingered on for more than a year. Early in 2000, the former mayor of Rotterdam – by then a government minister – was accused by the Rotterdam municipal council of having taken advantage of his position by submitting expense claims for things such as holidays, using his official car and chauffeur for private purposes, and so on. Of course the press eagerly took up the case and an enquiry was opened. Before the official report was published the minister resigned. Calling Holland too small a pond for a fish his size, he paid back those amounts he had received in illegitimate expenses, and more. After a cloudy investigation that – probably on purpose –

took months, the case was dropped – but not withdrawn. It was said that the loss of his job – and loss of face – were sufficient punishment. This wasn't totally satisfactory, of course, but the Dutch are used to a little hypocrisy in the field of 'egalitarianism'. Some are more equal than others, after all.... But at least the whole thing was brought to light.

The Dutch are aware of the rather narrow limits this attitude sets. If they find it all gets too much, they may use the term *spruitjeslucht* ('the smell of sprouts' – sprouts are a kind of cabbage.) Since on the one hand individual performance nowadays may be accompanied by more public pride and some privilege, while on the other a low profile is still widely appreciated, comments to the Rotterdam affair varied. Some took the view that 'You can hardly represent the world's largest port with a rowing boat, can you?', while others pointed out that this 'sumptuous representation' was paid for with public money.

One result of the affair was that parliament investigated the cost of all ministers' official cars. Many of them turned out to be more expensive than the norm set by law. Eyebrows were raised. One minister hastened to declare that his car had been taken over from his predecessor. Second-hand, so to speak. Luckily, the Prime Minister turned out to have one of the cheaper cars, well below the legal limit.... 'Cabbage smell' or not, the basic idea is still: no airs please, down to earth in a flat country.

Customer service? *'There is no customer service here, you need to beg for it!'* (Canada) This is another effect of egalitarianism that affects foreign visitors, although they may not recognise it as such. Many of the expatriates on my courses complain of poor customer service, saying things like: *'We have been struggling to get cable television installed for two months. They keep telling us they will come, but they never do. If we phone again, they say they will put our complaint in the computer, but all that hasn't done anything so far.'* (India) and: *'In restaurants here they let you wait for ages before a waiter shows up. In shops, the personnel stand around chatting to each other, occasionally looking at you, but not coming to assist you. They may also be very busy with paper work, but not with you as a customer'* (Britain). A young and quite low-profile English marketing(!) student told me: *'Now I've got used to it, but in the first weeks of my stay here I was quite shocked how shop personnel here just answer 'No' if you ask a question.'* Her fellow students from various countries all nodded their heads in recognition of her story....

This must indeed come across as strange (and rude, obviously) in a money-minded country where the provision of services produces a great part of the Gross National Product: banking, insurance, transport and consultancy are major economic activities. But on such a macro-economic scale, services, of course, are a product for which customers pay. At small-scale, individual levels as in shops and restaurants, service is an unpaid extra. Some foreigners add that it even works this way in their company: *'Sometimes the Dutch are annoyingly relaxed; take for instance the slow service between departments!'* (France)

There are various backgrounds to all this, but at the heart of it lies the fact that to the Dutch, customer service has a touch of hierarchy to it: the customer is a king and the personnel are 'low'. Hierarchical differences are hard to accept for the Dutch, making them feel uneasy and clumsy, and for this reason many of them cannot handle customer service. This also applies to many customers – they don't like it when an assistant approaches them immediately they enter the shop. They prefer to browse independently and simply walk out if they decide not to buy anything. As a result, good assistants are careful to not 'jump' on customers, bad ones just let the customer wait and then, if they are forced to offer assistance, give it in a rather curt way. Most foreigners, such as this American, are used to a different approach: *'Customer service here is terrible. I have the feeling that it is MY privilege to be THEIR customer. The attitude in the shops is not conducive to loyalty, that's for sure. I find myself thinking, 'Whew, I'll never go back THERE!' But then I find out that the next guy is just as haughty or rude. I'm sure that it's my fault, too. In America we believe that the customer is always right – regardless.'*

A contributing factor is probably the fact that shop personnel and waiters in restaurants have legal minimum wages and do not require tips to survive, as they do in the United States. Tipping is voluntary in Holland; all menus state that 'service is included'.[3]

Yet another reason may be that because of the relatively high wages they must pay, shops and restaurants employ as few staff as possible, so at peak times the assistants may simply be too busy to serve you. Supermarkets, cheaper restaurants, chain stores and the like usually employ young (=cheap!) assistants who do the job for only a short time and aren't deeply loyal to the company. In family-run shops and in more up-market firms, customer service is usually excellent and quite personal, which again is not to everyone's liking: *'The service is friendly but slow'* (Sweden). Others are more positive:

'*They are often multilingual and friendly in shops*' (Italy) A lot depends on the customers' own behaviour, too. If they are haughty in any way, acting in a superior manner, assistants will become obstinate. But if a customer asks for advice or help in an informal, low profile way, (subtlely stressing that any difference in position, lifestyle or income is purely coincidental) they will usually be met with a friendlier reaction. It isn't in everyone's character, of course, and I've heard terms like 'hypocritical' on this point, but all I can say is: just try it out and see for yourself.

So the Dutch try to ignore hierarchy, make it invisible as much as possible. The piece of advice I just gave will also work when dealing with service personnel at work and at home, such as the plumber. An example all the Dutch recognise is that when the cleaning lady arrives the 'employer' will do his/her best to avoid the idea that this simple work is 'low grade'. The former job title, 'the she-worker', was replaced decades ago by the more neutral word 'the help', and the Dutch usually clean up a bit *before* she comes.[4] Dutch people prefer not to be at home when the cleaning lady comes.

Having said all this, we should remember that egalitarianism is a value, that is, appreciated and acceptable behaviour. It does not mean that each and every Dutchman lives according to its tenets. But if they don't, they may expect criticism. The Dutch language has some twenty words and expressions for boasting and swaggering! The norms are strict: only in foreign contacts the Secretary of State for Economic Affairs may call him or herself the Minister of Trade. When in April 2000, accompanying the Crown Prince on a state visit to Japan, the lady who then held this office behaved as if she herself was royalty, it caused embarrassed giggling to the rest of the Dutch delegation.

And figures of authority, including royalty, have been fined by the police for breaking traffic regulations, and this deeply satisfies the nation: they're exactly like us, not any better. Just act normal!

All this does not imply that there *aren't* any 'higher' people, that there are no elite or authorities in the Netherlands. Of course there are, and they are recognisable to the general public by their appearance, the way they talk, their expensive cars and houses, etc. But in Holland such status is not taken for granted. In many places abroad, very expensive houses or even whole areas are surrounded by walls and other protective measures. Here, the rich prefer to live out of sight, tucked away behind trees. Ostentatious display of wealth is frowned upon, especially when the person involved can be classed as 'nouveau riche' and is regarded as lacking in style. A Dutchman who owned a Porsche (remember the Jaguar story…) told a television journalist that he doesn't enjoy driving this car on Dutch highways because people with slower cars either prevent him from using the fast lane, or offer insulting gestures, making clear he shouldn't think he is any better than them…. A particularly venomous comment could then be: 'Zandvoort-chic', referring to a not-very-posh bathing resort near Amsterdam. So, all in all, the rich and famous keep a rather low profile. This has its advantages too, because few people in Holland need bodyguards and the rich don't need to put up fences or walls around their houses, like they do elsewhere.

When passing through obviously well-to-do neighbourhoods, or seeing luxurious houses on TV, less fortunate people may well make some sour remark rather than an admiring comment. Of course there may be sheer jealousy involved, but there's always also a moral undertone of 'this is not quite right!'

Even for more sophisticated 'old money', wealth and power are something to be careful with, because to the Dutch they should be backed up by high moral standards, or at least with low-profile behaviour.

Class society   So under the surface of egalitarianism, the Netherlands is a class society after all, although perhaps a bit less visibly than some other European countries due to the low-profile attitudes. The fact that a person belongs to a particular class shouldn't be expressed too openly, so Dutch people have become experts in interpreting the signs: language (pronunciation, word usage, last names), dress, cultural tastes and general behaviour. To foreigners it may come as a shock: *'I was once refused help at a shop because the person working there 'did not think that I could afford' a Bang and Olufsen stereo. OK, so I was dressed like a bum.'* (USA)

Residence is an important indicator too: tell me your address and I can tell you quite accurately who you are. Towns, areas, streets and even parts of streets indicate one's wealth and place in society, and offer a fair chance of correctly estimating the educational level, income and cultural preferences. With strong social mobility in the last five decades, there is a status-driven hunt going on for 'better addresses', partly explaining the overheated housing market so much deplored by incoming expats.

In a rich country like Holland the *middle class* is predominant by far, both in numbers and public exposure, and has a gross annual income between (roughly) 30,000 and 70,000 euro. As in other western cultures subtle nuances among this large group, based on differences in income and expressed in lifestyle and status symbols, can be observed. Social control is quite strong in the Netherlands, and such differences are noticed and discussed, especially in 'suburbia' where many of these people live. The way you decorate your house and lay out your garden are visible indications of income and taste and so much money and attention is devoted to them. Ever-changing fashions make firms in these branches busy and prosperous, as can be seen from the large numbers of people visiting garden centres and 'furniture boulevards' at weekends and in the holidays.

There is still an *upper class* and the remains of a lower one. There is no true aristocracy in Holland and the upper class is largely made up of people who have either earned their money themselves or inherited it. Among themselves they may make the distinction between 'old' and 'new' money, but this is not openly commented upon in public. 'Old money' often lets itself be inspired by British examples, quiet and tasteful but ever so self-aware. The same American quoted above comments: *'I realise that the 'liberal' culture is sharply divided along class lines – in other words, the higher the class, the more conservative and closed-minded. It is not as liberal as I had thought.'* Many such people live in expensive areas, the ones house brokers lead house-hunting expats to: Wassenaar (The Hague area), Aerdenhout (Amsterdam/Haarlem), Hillegersberg (Rotterdam), Laren (Hilversum). Typical of Holland, a common characteristic of these places is that they are situated on sandy, slightly higher ground, not on swampy wet soils.

But there is a lot of 'new money' nowadays, with over 200,000 guilder-millionaires. 'New money' is often characterised by rather ostentatious consumerism, including flashy cars, of course, champagne breakfasts and other rather 'fancy', un-Dutch behaviour. Trying not to be cynical, I personally see this behaviour as a conscious attempt at dissociating itself from the 'grey masses', and from the norms and values of frugal parents and their old-time sober lifestyle. Originating from middle or lower class backgrounds but having the finances to imitate old money, many of them combine a supposedly 'grand' lifestyle with strong social control. Such people consider it important to drive the 'right' car, speak the 'right' language, be seen in the 'right' galleries and restaurants and at the 'right' parties and holiday destinations, and of course: to live in the 'right' places. They can admire themselves in certain magazines where the advertisements offer gadgets related to their patterns of consumption, while the editorials mildly mock them in their own terminology.

Because of social mobility, in the economic sense the *working class* these days has been replaced to a great extent by people from ethnic groups[5], although there still are some groups of Dutch blue-collar workers. They mostly live in the least privileged areas: the poor zones around the city centres dating from the 1890s, the suburbs of the 1950s and 60s meant to improve their housing conditions, and in the new towns a bit further afield. (A typical Dutch feature – as opposed to areas where rich people live, these were usually constructed in low, wet areas, former grasslands). City renovation has upgraded many of these neighbourhoods, but given high housing densities plus a population which is very mixed socially and ethnically, they are often still considered problematic to live in. Yet an American who asked me to show him a poor area in Amsterdam was rather amazed: *'You call* this *a poor area?'*. Some visitors think the complexes of tiny houses tucked away next to railway tracks are slums, but these are a kind of summer house with a garden, rented by city people.

Compared to nearby European countries Dutch working class areas are not really in bad shape, probably due to municipal authorities providing the same services to these neighbourhoods as to more prosperous areas.

Because rents are comparatively low such areas often have a high density of small shops, restaurants, galleries and the like, gradually turning some of them into fashionable and affordable places for students, artists and other less conformist people.

With social mobility and 'swapping' as a lifestyle, some people argue that the old class distinctions are fading away. A Dutch weekly[6] suggested a new division, based on lifestyles: 'Traditional commoners'; 'Modern commoners'; 'Convenience-oriented people'; 'The upward mobile'; 'Intellectuals'; 'Cosmopolitans'; 'Self-developers'; 'Post-materialists'. Unfortunately, the article didn't produce any real theory as to who fitted into which category.

Usage of names, greetings   In Dutch culture first names are not immediately used on first contact, unless the 'higher' party suggests so. For a while, people will address a new boss or customer as 'Mr X' or 'Mrs Y'. When the surname is used the formal you-word 'U' is employed, while the use of the first name automatically implies the informal you-word 'je'. In the seventies a general relaxation in manners led youngsters to almost always use first names and 'je', also to parents, teachers and other older people, but since about 1985 there seems to have been a reverse trend, certainly in business. Even when people introduce themselves with both first name and surname, others will be hesitant to use the first name right away if the other party is clearly senior in position or age. But in the work place, after perhaps a formal start, most people will use first names and 'je', even when those concerned are at quite different levels.

Making first acquaintances is always done with a handshake (firm but not overwhelmingly strong), as is done when meeting someone again after some time. But colleagues at work don't shake hands every day like the French tend to do. (A French lady comments: *'Here they say hallo all day long, to the same person!'*)

The two or even threefold cheek or air-kissing of the Dutch (by now famous among expatriates) is mostly restricted to private meetings. At work it may happen on birthdays and special occasions, between long-term colleagues. Women then kiss both sexes, men usually only the opposite sex, although in 'progressive' (not necessarily homosexual) circles this may now also be seen.

One strange aspect for many foreigners is that, unlike most countries, in Holland you answer the telephone, both at home and at work, by stating your name: 'Met (*with*) Jan de Vries', or 'Mevrouw (*Mrs.*) de Vries', either in a firm voice or a questioning one. The foreign way of just saying 'Hallo?' on the phone may lead to some confusion or even silence by the Dutch person on the other end: did I dial the right number? For those who prefer not use their family name at home, using first names only is an option.

Salaries Coming back to the subject of money, Dutch salary scales and the tax system also reflect the drive for equality. Just a few years ago research showed that Dutch managers and directors earned quite a bit less than comparable colleagues in other western countries, and that only in a very few countries was there a smaller difference between top salaries and bottom. Nowadays, in line with the 'hot' economy, top salaries are on the rise, and these may also be supplemented with performance bonuses and stock option packages. Even so, in an international perspective, earnings in the Netherlands are still fairly modest, and the gap between top and bottom salaries is still smaller than it is in quite a few other western countries. Yet in 1997, the Prime Minister criticised high managerial salaries. Employers paid him some lip service, but nothing has really changed so far. When in July 2000 it became known that top managers' salaries had risen on average by 13% in 1999 (in addition to their stock option profits), the trade unions immediately complained. They asked what these managers had done so much better than the workers who had received only a small rise in the same period. The matter was also widely debated in the media and in parliament even the party most popular among entrepreneurs agreed that it was not a wise policy and that it was a threat to the harmony of the Dutch model. Yet at Christmas 2000, the Dutch newspaper *NRC-Handelsblad* wrote: 'The poor are less poor, the rich much richer'.

Salaries are private   In Holland salaries are regarded as a highly personal matter, both in public and in private. Up until the present time Dutch companies have not been legally obliged to publish the salaries -let alone the perks- of their top managers, and they don't. However, under pressure from the trade unions, this may soon change, since in the Dutch model controlled wages are crucial and employees want to ensure it's not only *them* who are restraining themselves financially. With Dutch companies buying foreign firms more and more often, it is known that foreign executives now employed by Dutch companies often earn quite a bit more than their Dutch bosses. But for the time being, informally and at lower levels it is taboo, and will probably remain taboo, to ask anyone, even relatives and friends, how much they earn! Your Dutch friends and colleagues may try to find out your salary, and if you don't tell them they'll draw their own conclusions from your pattern of consumption.

Taxes as a levelling factor   The tax system helps to ensure net salaries do not differ too much: before 2001, top income was still taxed at a 60% rate, almost twice that of lower salaries. The Dutch tax system has some unique features, such as total tax deduction of mortgage interest (a 'holy cow' in Dutch politics!), which also makes life more bearable for people with high incomes. In 1999 it was calculated that, in spite of the top rate of 60%, at 43% of the GNP the average tax burden was lower than that in Scandinavia, Germany, France and Belgium.

But important tax changes have been made. As of January 2001 all rates have been reduced, so that people get to keep more of their earnings, thus making work more attractive. At the same time taxes on consumption have been raised. The top rate has been decreased to 52%. To make the whole plan budget-neutral, private wealth over a certain level will remain taxable, while VAT has gone up from 17.5 to 19%. (For the peace of mind of non-Dutch readers it should be mentioned that people working temporarily in the Netherlands enjoy a tax exemption of 35%. And for foreign investors investing in Holland the tax climate is so favourable that the European Commission has accused the country of playing unfairly in intra-European competition!) Needless to say, quite a few people look for ways of evading taxes and it is estimated that the 'black' economy runs into several billion Euros. Foreign tax constructions may enjoy some popularity among people whose work involves activities abroad, yet one cannot say that tax evasion is rampant. Practical reasons for this may be that the well-organised Dutch bureaucracy makes it difficult to do so, and that a good accountant can still find interesting legal loopholes. Probably a more important reason is that the tax system is in accordance with the Dutch core-value of egalitarianism. In broad outline, it is considered fair and honest. In the 1990s, The Dutch Inland Revenue launched a new public approach under the slogan 'We can't make it nicer, but we can make it more simple', accompanied with entertaining (!) radio and TV -spots and clear explanations of the altogether complicated system. The whole campaign was a success, even winning great appreciation for the tax system from the general public. Electronic tax forms (with built-in calculations and deductions etc.) that can be submitted through Internet have already been successful for some years.

And everyone can see what is done with the taxes, for their own comfort and benefit and that of others. Although in recent years government policy has encouraged a free market approach, many public facilities are still subsidised: public transport, education at all levels, classical music concerts, theatre groups, museums, libraries, facilities for the disabled, housing schemes, house rents for low-income earners, and many more things. All this costs billions each year, but it is generally accepted that they are all good reasons for paying taxes. Other major tax expenditure is on social benefits for unemployment, ill health, old age, etc. By international standards these benefits are very generous. They are part of Dutch culture. It is generally felt that it's not their own fault that people find themselves in such situations, and that they should therefore be given the chance to 'act normal', too. It also makes the country a more pleasant place for the taxpayers to live in. Poverty, people not insured against illness and social upheaval in general, are phenomena largely unknown in Holland and when social problems do occur financial inequality is not generally the root cause.

Foreigners are quite often surprised by this. In the first edition of this book I quoted a Czech, who, just before the communist system in his country collapsed, said: *'The Netherlands is more socialist than the 'socialist' countries'*. Mentioning this quote to Hungarian and Polish course participants just recently, they agreed with the comparison between the Dutch system and former communism. The Czech added: *'The way they take care of the weak here! Take ill people for example: one may be ill for some weeks a couple of times a year, they just keep paying you. The unemployed get benefits and something extra for their holidays. It is very social here, in some respects too much, which causes people to abuse it easily.'* Well, these conditions did not change, so small wonder that in 2000 a Turkish manager commented: *'Karl Marx would be quite happy here.'* And a German intellectual working in Holland said: *'The fact that badly disabled people get the cost of visiting a prostitute reimbursed by the health service proves to me that Holland is a very social country. (...) I find it unbelievably good that such a thing is possible.'*

Of course no one likes receiving the blue tax envelopes, but all in all the Dutch public feels the system is right. Most people silently agree that justice and social harmony are well worth paying for. Then we can all act normal.

The historical origins of egalitarianism   It is now time to look at the origins of this core-value of Dutch culture. The sense of being morally equal originates from, and at the same time perpetuates, the rather flat pyramid of Dutch society. In his book 'Culture's Consequences', Geert Hofstede[7] indicates that what he names 'Power Distance' in the Netherlands is among the lowest in the world, only surpassed in the Scandinavian countries.

Hofstede puts this down largely to the Protestant nature of Dutch society. I agree and shall come back on this later. But many foreign observers point to even older roots. They see the Dutch natural environment as the origin of this low hierarchy. It is highly controversial, of course, to directly link a nation's mentality to its scenery or climate, but there is indeed a striking similarity: flat country, flat society. Some stress the fact that in a low-lying country such as Holland, with large areas of reclaimed land, everyone is threatened equally by water. Water is a very democratic element indeed. But others object, pointing out that other regions threatened by water – Bangladesh, the Nile Delta, parts of China – aren't equality-minded at all! The explanation, however, might be found in a related aspect: the unique social structures that the Dutch developed to fight the everlasting threat of water.

The water control boards (*waterschappen*), that cover the whole country nowadays, were founded as long ago as the 13th century and are therefore older than virtually all other public institutions. Since a central government hardly existed in those days, people threatened by water had to rely on their own initiative for survival. These self-help-organisations consisted of a group of farmers or fishermen who chose a leader from their own ranks and were therefore very flat in structure. The elected *dijkgraaf* (literally: the count of the dyke) was in fact a 'primus inter pares' who could only exercise power when high tides or threatening storms made it necessary. For centuries, all (male) inhabitants of the region covered by the *waterschap* had to contribute to the construction, guarding and repair of the dykes. Since all had a vested interest in doing so, they contributed manpower and finance. Thus, people made themselves so to speak 'physically autonomous' in a structure with a very low hierarchy. (Nowadays the *waterschappen* are highly professional organisations, and the *dijkgraaf* is an engineer, but he – or she – is still elected and taxes are still levied from anyone living in their territory).

On a more philosophical level, other factors contributed to egalitarianism. Here we come back to Protestantism. Before the Reformation, as early as the late 1300s, a religious movement ('The Brethren of Common Life') in the then Catholic Low Countries called for a sober, spiritually-oriented existence rather than the luxurious way of life that had developed among the clergy. A hundred years later, Erasmus' Humanism pleaded for humane, righteous and non-violent behaviour to all living souls, including animals. Ideas such as these did indeed influence Dutch Protestantism and later permeated society as more and more people received some form of general education.

In the mid-1500s Calvinism (a particularly strict version of protestant Christian faith) became the dominant religion. It emphasised that all people are born imperfect, prone to sin, and that one should work all one's life on improving oneself in order to persuade God to forgive our original sin. On a moral level, disregarding one's social position, all people are equally bad, brothers and sisters in sin. In the Bible, Jesus indicates that a wealthy or powerful person can be a greater sinner at heart than a repentant thief or a prostitute. Everyone, therefore, should scrutinise his own behaviour for the flaws of sin, and work on them. It was a call for individual soul-searching rather then for collective expressions of faith; for quiet and thoughtful thinking rather than emotional outbursts or extravagant group behaviour. Protestant religion focuses on *contents*, on The Word of God, not on form and ritual. This can be felt throughout protestant northwestern Europe. In the Netherlands, up to this day, Calvinistic churches are quite empty; undecorated and white as they are on the inside, they stimulate an individualistic mood of introspection.

All in all, one's task on earth – and towards God – was considered more important and more lasting than any worldly appearance or position. Consequently, Calvinism also stressed the need to think of others. The biblical expression of this state of mind – 'Do unto others as you would have them do unto you' – is still heard in Holland.[8] It stimulates social awareness and charity, and keeps us from selfishly pursuing our own interests. Of course this soul-searching also led to the scrutinising of others, to moralism, and to long and fierce debate about what then was the right attitude, the correct interpretation. This contents-orientation permeates Dutch thinking and mentality to the present day.

The dividing line between Protestantism and Catholicism in the Netherlands roughly coincides with the one between the wetter and drier parts of the country. A rather vague coherence, it seems. In my opinion, the rapid spread of Calvinistic socio-religious equality and autonomy was related to the physical autonomy that the lowlanders had accomplished with their waterworks. Let me present modern evidence of this idea. Every year on the occasion of Queen's day, the Queen bestows various types of royal decoration on virtuous citizens (*lintjesregen* or 'the badge rain'). In April 2000, it was found out that these decorations are awarded more frequently in the higher and drier' Catholic' south than in the 'Protestant' north. An odd division, it seems, but since local people nominate such citizens to the Crown, I think this proves my point: in the Catholic, less egalitarian south, people attach more importance to this prestigious tradition than people in the lower, wetter provinces up north which were traditionally Protestant.

To finish this short historical overview of religion: Calvinism became a leading force in the political struggle that gained the Dutch independence from Habsburg Spain. In all but name Calvinism reached the status of a state religion, while Catholicism had to go into hiding. Calvinism maintained its dominant position[9] until about 1850, when a church rift divided the Protestants into two separate denominations, later followed by others. At the same time, Catholics were allowed to surface again, and were soon followed by the emerging socialist movement.

Religion remained a highly influential factor in Dutch society up to about 1960. Then social changes, which resulted in the rejection of existing power structures, rather suddenly eroded religion, turning the modern-day Netherlands into one of the least church-going nations of Europe: only one in four Dutch people regularly visits any Christian church these days. Except for some ceremonies such as royal weddings, the Christian religion has mostly disappeared from public life; it is a private matter now, to be discussed rather discreetly. (All this is far less true for the followers of Islam, but I will discuss them in chapter 11, which deals with the large immigrant population.)

On the other hand, apparently there are many Dutch people still in search of spiritual values. All kinds of Asian religions and new-age movements have followers and students in Holland: in 1999 the number of (native Dutch!) Buddhists was estimated at some 120,000. Even the more traditional churches claim that youngsters, unhampered by aversion to the traditions, are expressing a new interest in religion.

True Calvinism nowadays encompasses only some 8% of the population, most of them rural[10], yet its concept of moral equality still permeates many aspects of Dutch society and behaviour. Religion may have lost a lot of its importance, but its related values linger on.

Now that you are aware of the general mood in the country, let us turn towards work and business and see how this affects everyday behaviour and the relationships between people at different levels.

1. This also relates to a certain degree of collectivism that people appreciate in their own circle. We will come to this in a later chapter.

2. By Bureau Trendbox BV, Amsterdam.

3. In fact, the Dutch usually DO tip, by 'rounding up' the bill. About 5 to 10% is usual – but tipping is considered a friendly gesture, not a kind of 'social duty' as it is in the USA.

4. In cities, nowadays some 'helps' are male, often East-European students.

5. See chapter 9.

6. *HP-De Tijd*, February 2000.

7. Geert Hofstede is considered the 'guru' of cross-cultural studies. He is the most quoted Dutch scientist internationally.

8. Two linguists discovered that in present-day Dutch some 800 biblical expressions are still regularly used, albeit without people realising their religious origins.

9. Not in the southern provinces of Brabant and Limburg, see chapter 10.

10. See chapter 10.

Chapter 4

HIERARCHICAL ISSUES
IN EVERYDAY WORKING LIFE

So 'acting normal' is the appreciated standard and the Dutch seem to have a problem accepting hierarchy. What effect does this have in companies and organisations, where people have different degrees of authority, power and status? How are decisions taken when everybody is supposedly the same in theory, but obviously not so in practice?

I am aware that to readers from other European countries and to people working in large and internationally operating companies, the general outline of the methods employed and the solutions reached, which I describe below, may not always be surprising. But even for them, some details of the everyday working situation in Holland will, I trust, be new and unusual. And in my experience Dutch work-culture can certainly confuse people from other parts of the world and from less globally oriented enterprises and organisations.

The previous chapter mostly described situations in private life in the Netherlands, or situations related to government circles and politics. With levels of ambition and competition in the Dutch business world rising, the core value of egalitarianism may be a little less noticeable nowadays than it used to be, but it certainly still has its effects. Let us look first at the everyday atmosphere in the work place and then widen the scope to look at what is behind it legally.

The general mood   Egalitarianism still plays an important role in personal relations at work. The Dutch are task-oriented, as we shall see in a later chapter, and under normal circumstances hierarchy shouldn't play a role. Employees in lower positions should not be treated as 'subordinates', as inferiors who only do what their boss tells them to. Dutch workers are (usually) responsible and hard-working. They like to work on their task independently, without being checked up on all the time. Unlike in some countries, they will continue to work just as hard even when the boss is not present. Everyone's contribution is important to the quality of the finished 'product' and therefore a manager, supervisor or foreman should consult and discuss rather than order people around. By being open and approachable, superiors make not only themselves more acceptable but also the hierarchy, which is unavoidable but slightly embarrassing to the Dutch. Some humour and a personal approach also help a great deal. Typical examples of this might be company directors queuing up in the company canteen, just like anyone else, or gallantly inviting personnel to enter the elevator before them. (By the way, unlike in some other countries, Dutch firms usually only have one single restaurant or canteen, for personnel at all levels. As an exception visiting VIPs may be served lunch in the boardroom) Moreover, few executives openly call themselves 'director' or any similar term. Others might use the term but they themselves would probably jokingly reply 'Well, at least that's what they call me.'

Superiors with such a management style – 'human', friendly, not merely 'using' their personnel in a functional capacity, not assuming privileges while among personnel – will be able to count on the loyal co-operation of the workforce in busy, difficult or stressful circumstances.

Dealing with Dutch secretaries

To begin with, a German quote: *'Before long, my secretary was calling me Fritz. That took quite some getting used to.'*

To get the best out of a Dutch secretary, who virtually without exception will be a woman[1], it is advisable to keep a low profile and not be 'bossy'. A good working relationship requires mutual trust in ability, capacity and responsibility, concern about each other's working methods and workload. Your Dutch secretary prefers to be your efficient window on the company and buffer against the outside world, rather than someone who does little more than type letters and make the coffee. She wants to be proud of her job, thinking along your lines and feeling that your success is hers too.

In companies employing managers from other countries I have heard Dutch secretaries complain about the 'aloofness' and 'arrogance' of their new boss, who 'orders them around'. In order to avoid your secretary feeling this way, involve her as far as possible in your everyday schedule and plan future work together. This will allow her to operate at maximum efficiency and effectiveness. Let her know who your contacts are and how important these are for the business. She should be acquainted with your personal management style so she can 'smooth out the bumps' if necessary. Remember that she has probably been around in the company longer than you so, especially in the beginning, ask her advice on issues before you take action, enquire how things are done and how to approach people in the most effective way. To ensure smooth co-operation some openness about your family affairs and private interests is important and this will be reciprocated. It indicates that both boss and secretary are just people, too. It is also advisable to treat the administrative workers below her in more or less the same way.

The 'OR'   Dutch directors and general managers are quite aware of the limits 'moral egalitarianism' sets on their exercise of authority. Since their staff and personnel are usually well educated and fully realise their importance to the company, they demand – and get – a say in its affairs. Employees will speak up when things are not to their liking, not only when it concerns details such as the whereabouts of the coffee machine, but also in far more decisive matters. Equal rights and respect for all levels of the workforce are reflected in the phenomenon of the company council, which is quite normal in Europe, but not in other countries: *'I admire your law on company councils. To American standards it is unbelievable that (...) a representative organ of workers can criticise the management and stop certain decisions.'* (USA)

In the Netherlands every company with more than 35 employees is legally required to have a workers' council (called OR in its Dutch abbreviation, pron. oh-air)[2] Under normal circumstances this system of company-democracy generally functions quite well. Members of the OR are elected by their fellow-workers every couple of years, and the employer is legally obliged to allow them to be trained for their council activities during work hours. Trade unions play a role in the background but are not directly involved. (At about 25% unionisation in Dutch industry is fairly low, although it is somewhat higher in other branches such as education, health care and public administration.)

At department levels there are what the Dutch literally call 'work-discussions' (*werk-overleg,* regular team meetings discussing work progress and new projects. On a more personal level 'performance-talks' (*functioneringsgesprekken)* are held, individual evaluative talks in which the lower and higher level employee can <u>mutually</u> vent their comments on each other's performance, general behaviour and attitudes. Wishes and decisions on new tasks and projects can also be discussed. A short report is then written and signed by both participants. They each keep a copy and one more copy is passed on to the personnel department.

The result of all these talks and agreements is that in most Dutch companies and institutions there is a constant flow of information on policy, planning, procedures and results – and this flow is not only from top to bottom. Obviously these procedures are not to everyone's liking because they can distract from the day-to-day tasks involved in running the business and, of course, there is also criticism on the quality, legibility and length of all these papers and meetings. But when all is said and done they are seen in a positive light as a good thing for all involved. All the parties know where they stand and most people are convinced that they have a positive affect on the way the company functions, and on everyone's position within it.

CAO   Another important aspect of egalitarianism in companies is to be found in workers' labour conditions. As they do in most west-European countries (but not in others), people at middle and lower working levels generally come under what is called a collective labour agreement (*Collectieve Arbeidsovereenkomst*, CAO, pron. say-ah-oh). Larger companies have their own CAO, smaller firms in a particular branch have a joint one. The CAOs are the outcome of annual or bi-annual negotiations between the employer(s), trade union represen-tatives and government officials. The CAO contains all kinds of regula-tions on issues such as safety, holidays, clothing, working hours, etc. etc., but most of all, of course, on wages and salaries. The CAO is valid for all workers, including for non-union members.

Although agreeing to the CAO offers workers great security and protection it takes away their individual right to demand other perks – but companies are free to offer more than the CAO requires. Obviously the CAO system decreases competition between workers, which is incomprehensible to some foreign (especially American) managers, but the point is it satisfies the Dutch need for equal treatment and equal opportunities. The older generations tend to see the CAO system as the positive outcome of social democracy, of their struggle for better working conditions.

For a long time the trade unions turned down management pro-posals for payment by performance. That would stimulate competi-tion between workers, and of course that was not acceptable or desirable to more egalitarian-oriented workers' organisations. But times are changing: in a survey carried out in the summer of the year 2000, it turned out that 48% of those interviewed were actually in favour of some method of payment by performance, with just 20% adamantly against. In that year's CAO agreements about 40% of Dutch companies and organisations had already included arrangements for some degree of differential payment on top of the basic salaries. This makes it likely that sooner or later this system will be introduced elsewhere – but it will not be without resistance. In a radio debate on the issue people wondered how it would work out in non-profit sectors such as health care and education, where quality should come before quantity.

All in all, in the present booming economy, with its high demand for labour all kinds, more and more people (especially youngsters) are tending, on a more individual basis, to give up some security in exchange for higher wages and other attractive working conditions. This means that to the chagrin of the unions the number of people working under CAO agreements – or belonging to a union at all, for that matter – is gradually decreasing. A related effect is that public bodies at all levels are having a hard time finding people to fill their vacancies, which are perceived as offering more security than the private sector but also fewer financial incentives and less challenge.

Being in charge   The general mood in Dutch companies and organisations is that whether we are a boss or a worker, in the end we are all human and we all do our best. As a result of workers' input through the OR, people at all levels have a high degree of responsibility and involvement – at least they are supposed to. Power games or compulsion are therefore unusual and unwanted. Dutch managers and supervisors are not in a position to shake their fist and say: 'I'm the boss, this is what I want doing and all of you must just get on and do it!' In interviews carried out in August 2000 at the expat web site Expatica[3], Dutch people with working experience in the United States called the management styles there 'dictatorial' and even 'militaristic'. I have heard similar strong terms during my research visits to Dutch expats in very different continents....

In the Netherlands, bosses and managers are supposed to gain authority through their expertise and clever strategies, not as the result of company hierarchy. Anyone attempting to 'play the big boss' would first be met by giggles of disbelief at such outlandish behaviour

('What on earth is the matter with him this morning?'). If he persisted individual workers or even the entire department would fiercely protest at such attempted coercion and possibly try to sabotage this 'authoritarianism'. If the conflict is more structural employees will immediately involve the OR, of course.

Saying that authority depends on expertise sounds as if a person in charge should know everything. That is not the case; in Dutch culture it is no shame not to have an immediate answer ready to questions an employee, or anyone else, might ask. Over the last decades, Dutch education has not focused on students knowing hard facts and on learning things by heart, on having the 'right' answer always at hand. Rather, it has tried to stimulate students to be interested in things, to formulate good questions and then be creative in finding answers to them, through books, people, the Internet, or any other source. In this complex modern world it is impossible to know everything. This is reflected in the Dutch manager's attitude that telling someone 'I don't know, but I'll find out for you' does not lead to loss of face. In Dutch culture asking for information is not a sign of weakness. They will find out, either themselves or by asking other people, and then come back to you with the answer.

In line with world-wide developments, the Dutch manager is not seen as a schoolteacher who tells everyone what to do, but as an inspiring leader who should give direction and vision to a team consisting of people who – in return – are also supposed to come up with creative and productive ideas. The manager should know the overall line, and give protection to the team, that is how 'expertise' should be defined.

Now this may be many a company's ideal, but of course reality isn't always perfect. In the Netherlands, too, there are still 'bossy' bosses, conceited little dictators or self-willed loners, managers who are better at talking than at listening. But given the outspokenness of many Dutch workers, the chances are they will be met with more bottom-upwards resistance than they would in many other countries.

If the company hits hard times and a tougher personnel policy is inevitable, management must – and will – always involve the OR in discussions. It would also be a wise policy to explain the difficult situation seriously to the workers in more direct ways, asking for their co-operation in solving the problems in an atmosphere of mutual trust and loyalty. Working together with the OR, management will attempt to soften any unpleasant, but necessary, measures. There have been examples of employees working extra hours without pay to help the company to survive. If cutting down the workforce is inevitable, a solution involving a shorter working week for everyone rather than dismissing people may be found. If job losses are inevitable, they may be made through 'natural discharge'.[4] Other solutions may be early retirement for older or sick workers, outplacement facilities for people leaving voluntarily and 'golden handshakes' for higher management (Note that there is a hierarchy after all!). Finally, if all these measures fail to overcome the company's problems, mass dismissals may only take place after consultations with the trade unions involved followed by legal approval.

When the going gets rough many companies and organisations in Holland – more so than in other countries – involve external troubleshooters and *interim* managers to solve conflicts and restructure things. This is booming business, since outsiders can more successfully implement unwelcome changes than people from inside a company, no matter what their position.

Reshuffling   Until recently few individuals were publicly admonished, let alone punished, as a result of organisational reshuffling. In Dutch culture, it is preferred to seek the source of failure in procedures[5] rather than in individual actions – in other words: through an analysis of how people and organisations co-operate. These days public scapegoating of top people does happen more often, both in business and in government. But even then those held responsible for the problem are removed as elegantly as possible, with golden handshakes, or moved to more neutral positions as 'advisors'. Some foreigners living here are dismayed about the way this works: *'Time and again in the past few years my jaw has dropped as I have watched corrupt or incompetent officials step down after their misdeeds have been found out, without having to face prosecution, as high functionaries are not even brought to book for gambling with public funds.'* (USA) Yes, in a small-scale society such as Holland striving for harmony may lead to this extreme situation. (By the way, in 2000 the Netherlands was listed as the world's ninth least corrupt nation – a slightly worse position than previously…). Of course people at lower levels bitterly comment that the big-shots all cover up for each other, as they do in all countries, but such storms usually blow over. Only a few individuals who have been truly exposed as malfunctioning have chosen to leave the country, at least for a period. Some have given interviews or written a book defending their views and actions.

It should be said that given the thriving economy there is not that much really bad news these days. Company closures and bankruptcies are rare. The general trend in recent years, as elsewhere, has been a flattening of organisations, a breaking up into smaller, semi-independent departments which have more autonomy in deciding their own affairs. Workers' involvement has thus been reinforced rather than diluted. This is especially so because many of them now own shares in their company. Given the great demand for good managers, companies now offer bonuses both to attract such people and to keep them. At the same time, golden handshakes as a device for getting rid of not-so-effective managers have become higher and higher, but just like salaries their levels tends to be hushed up.

Dismissals   One more effect of egalitarianism in the labour market can be found in the procedures for dismissing people. Sacking employees is not all that straightforward in the Netherlands, although there is more flexibility now, given the higher job-mobility and the better chance of people dismissed of finding another job. Yet, Dutch law as a whole still reflects the country's egalitarian values. Through the CAOs, Dutch labour legislation strongly supports employees and protects those in vulnerable positions from injustice and arbitrariness. Only in a few specific cases (bare-faced theft and such like) may employees be sacked on the spot. In any less simple labour conflict workers will fight their dismissal in court (backed up by free legal assistance and/or trade union support) because if they don't they will lose their right to unemployment benefit. Since the employee is almost automatically considered 'the weaker party' judges often tend to take their side by prohibiting dismissal or by granting them some kind of bonus. For people not covered by a CAO dismissal is, of course, easier, since they chose a higher risk job.

Résumés (curriculum vitae)   When people are hired, too, the Dutch tendency towards low-profile behaviour may be apparent. Most Dutch people are afraid that if they include every last detail about their studies and work experience in their curriculum vitae they will be considered boastful or arrogant.

They may just briefly list their qualifications and experience, expecting the people carrying out the job interview to have read between the lines and pose questions designed to extract further details. The result may be that you, as a foreigner used to more confident or extensive curriculum vitae, may think little of an application while your Dutch colleagues may think that person worth interviewing. Of course the same low-profile behaviour – over-modest self-presentation – may occur during a personal interview. Recently some Dutch educational institutions have started teaching their students how to 'sell' themselves better by writing an eye-catching résumé or speaking more confidently. Long-term unemployed people can learn the same technique at special training institutes which have been set to get such people back on track.

Flexibility   In the face of growing international competition and in line with general European labour regulations, Dutch companies and the government have worked hard at creating a more flexible labour market. Since dismissals (of the majority under CAO-regulated contract) are complicated, lengthy and costly procedures, companies are increasingly wary of hiring people on a permanent basis. The 'slimmed-down organisation' is therefore a popular concept. These organisations are characterised by a high degree of automation and computerisation rather than in a large number of staff members.

Temporary workers are brought in to bridge peak periods. Hired through temp agencies, they can be dismissed far more easily. The proportion of temp workers in Holland is one of the highest in the world – one reason being that part-time working is popular (see chapter 8). It is one of the pillars of the polder model. In many Dutch high streets the sign *Uitzendbureau* – (temporary) employment agency – proliferates. These organisations started decades ago as pools of administrative workers, but by now they also provide people for jobs requiring higher qualifications, including computer experts, *interim* managers, and so on. The legal and tax position of temp workers is strengthened by the *uitzendbureaus* who offer these people permanent work contracts with them, while the actual work is carried out in client organisations. This is a booming business and some firms in the field are successfully expanding in neighbouring countries, where attempts to copy the Dutch polder model have resulted in the creation of a level playing field.

All in all, Dutch labour legislation is gradually changing, as younger generations with a different system of values move up in the business world. Flexible work schedules and greater differences in salary are increasingly being considered normal and accepted. In some branches, especially the ICT sector and related fields, the demand for workers is so urgent that companies will do anything to get personnel. Airline tickets and mobile phones are given away, simply to get young people interested. Job applications are organised to resemble fun TV shows and if people accept the job they can negotiate 'tertiary labour conditions', such as four-days-a-week contracts, facilities for childcare, sabbaticals[6], etc. In general, when one considers this differentiation in salaries and perks, the traditional concept of material egalitarianism seems to have been weakened. But the non-material attitude of 'just act normal' is still with us, as I hope to make clear below.

Stakeholders and shareholders   Yet another aspect of egalitarianism in the Dutch business world is the fact that stakeholders' value (rather than just shareholders') is still considered quite important. The message is that one should invest wisely and calmly, not just for the purpose of making a quick profit but for fully engaging in the well-being of the company, where the position of workers, the talents of the managers and the interests of both clients, contractors and any other party involved should all be given serious attention. Many people still find this the preferred, decent attitude. A quote from a British executive with a wide experience in working internationally: *'The big difference is that* (name of company) *and its activities are truly a part of this society. In many countries where I've worked, in a few discussions you could convince people of the use of your plans (…). Here things don't work that way. You have to do with the* polder model, *with a series of organisations, the environmental movement, and politics. You're being taken through all of society, so to speak, a difficult but fascinating process.'*

One particular version of this may be the trend toward 'ethical entrepreneurship' or 'responsibility management' that is now to be found in some major Dutch companies. Copying American examples, many now have 'mission statements' to describe their usefulness to society, and 'codes of conduct' in which they – largely with an eye on critical consumers and the media- declare that they are aiming for production processes which not harmful to the environment at home or in far away countries, do not employ child labour or impose abusive conditions on adult workers and have nothing to do with corruption or other questionable practices. (Not all Dutch firms live by such lofty principles; even after press campaigns – one company openly refused to withdraw from its economic involvement with Burma's military dictatorship.)

In spite of all this, in line with what seems to be an increased 'Americanisation' of Dutch society, owning shares and playing the stock market has become a widespread phenomenon over the last few years. Driven by media hype and other peoples' stories, quite a few people – and not only the rich – are greedily trying to cash in, not caring very much about the stakeholders.

Early in 2000, a large Internet provider, WorldOnline, was floated on the stock market. After an aggressive media campaign promising sky-high profits, many people eagerly paid the high price that was set by the bank responsible for the flotation. From the very beginning, however, the share price went down and down. When it then became known that the company's founder had sold part of her shareholding *before* the official flotation, all the new shareholders complained loudly and bitterly. A few months later the company was taken over by an Italian firm at a knockdown price. As I write this, it is not yet known what the legal consequences of the whole affair will be, but financial experts, lawyers and – again! – the media moralistically commented that this only proved yet again that greed leads to misery. And, of course, there were demands for stricter control – see chapter 5.

In Dutch society trying to get rich quick by playing the stock market is sometimes still depicted as unwise and slightly immoral speculation, something to be frowned upon. There is an old saying in Dutch which can be translated roughly as 'arrogance leads to a fall'. This was again illustrated in comments on the whole affair: both the semi-legal machinations of the woman who had founded the company and the naked greed of the investors trying to make a quick profit were roundly condemned. Once again the message was: Act normal, don't try too hard to out-compete other people, and everything will be fine.

Representation   People don't act normal all the time, of course, certainly not when they want to make a good impression. With financial affluence, the growing importance of public relations, and perhaps in imitation of the American style of business, the issue of representation has gained enormous attention in recent years. Owning a 'sky-box' in a football stadium, in which favoured suppliers, clients and customers can be entertained, has been fashionable for some years, and it is becoming increasingly customary to give such people VIP treatment at great public and sporting events.[7]

This attention may last just half a day, sometimes, which may be quite normal for some cultures, but it strikes people from other parts of the world, where the representation may be less costly but more personal and for a longer time. In turn, that might make individualistic Dutch business people, pressed for time as they are, a bit uneasy...

On a more everyday level, the following American (!) observation might be interesting: *'I am absolutely amazed to see how much money Dutch companies spend on lavish brochures, business cards, office space, art for their walls – and parties! Wow – you don't see that in the U.S.'* Indeed, in recent years high-level representation has become a major issue – and big business! The amount and quality of company advertising provide PR companies, graphic designers, printers and distributors with an excellent living. But don't think Dutch companies spend these vast amounts of money frivolously. The cost-effectiveness of such campaigns is carefully worked out beforehand, and if they do not live up to expectations they are quickly reduced in scale or even abandoned altogether.

Customer service, once again   Several of the circumstances mentioned above help to lower the degree of customer service still further. In the public sector, especially, it is difficult to reach people during lunch or coffee breaks. Colleagues in a particular department may all choose to have a coffee break at the same time, so that there is no-one to answer incoming telephone calls. The rationale – perhaps logical but nonetheless arrogant – is: 'If it's really important, they'll phone back'. Luckily, the Dutch usually take short lunch breaks, see chapter 6.

Another problem is that when you phone such an organisation it may take ages before you are connected to the right department. In many cases you will have to work your way through automatic answering procedures telling you – in Dutch! – to dial 2 for this information and 3 for an answer to that question. And when you finally get through to a real live human being, to your enormous irritation the phrase 'one moment, please' usually signifies a five-minute wait. Obviously employers don't like this, and often organise customer service training programmes for their employees. But after an initial improvement, matters usually return to 'normal'. An article in a Dutch newspaper gave the following hint: phone at 8.05 a.m. so that you are the first, or one of the first, caller, and if you have to wait too long, dial again but change the last three numbers, so as to reach another department in the same organisation. The manner in which private companies deal with customers on the telephone is usually a little better than that described for public organisations, but even there it is often far from perfect.

1. See chapter 10 on gender issues.
2. For detailed factual and legal information on this and other labour regulations, refer to 'Employers and Labour Relations in the Netherlands', a 1998 publication by the Dutch General Employers' Association AWVN. It can be ordered by transferring 20 guilders (9 euro) to postal bank account 50194 of AWVN, Haarlem. P.O.Box 568, 2003 RN Haarlem, the Netherlands. Tel. (**) 023 - 5101 213/215, web site www.awvn.nl
3. www.expatica.com
4. People leaving the company are not replaced by new personnel, more on this in chapter 7.
6. For readers from countries that do not know this phenomenon: sabbatical periods (a few months or even a full year) are highly appreciated, unpaid, long-term leave, with a guarantee of returning to your job afterwards. Many people use a sabbatical for further study, world travel, or other time consuming private activities.
7. See chapter 8.

Chapter 5

DIRECTNESS AND CRITICISM

'Straight through the sea'
(Dutch saying praising directness)

The Dutch have a reputation for being very direct in their speech and their approach – remember the curt answer 'No' in shops. The reactions of people participating in my course range from the positive *'confident'*, through rather neutral terms such as *'straightforward'* and *'very honest,'* to the less positive *'abrupt'*, *'blunt'* and *'rude'*. People from abroad are usually shocked at first but after they have been here for a while many come to appreciate this directness. Of course it also depends on what they are used to in their own culture.

Most Dutch people are not even aware of this directness. They feel that since all people are more or less equal, so are their ideas. In Dutch society, everyone has the right to say what they think, no matter their social position, so opinions are easily voiced. In working life and general society most people have a rather functional approach to others: you want something, I can provide it; both of us are here to do a job; you are a customer, I am a vendor. Personal characteristics don't matter too much in such a transactional relationship. Content please, not form. Yes is yes and no is no.

Any personal aspect such as mutual liking or humour may be a pleasant extra, but is not strictly necessary to do business or to carry out a transaction. (This is probably one reason foreigners complain about a certain 'coldness' in the Dutch.) So in the workplace not much attention is paid to outward signs of respect, even when others are around, people speak up to their superiors and feel free to disagree with them – unless it's on sensitive (usually personal) issues. The words *'yes, but …'* are fairly standard in most Dutch conversations.

Provided such opinions and comments are given in a calm, rational way they are also listened to – although they are certainly not always accepted! But no one need fear, sanctions are not likely to follow, although you may be frankly criticised in return! Superiors cannot really put someone down for merely stating his or her opinion, and although it happens sometimes of course, people are not supposed to use other people as stepping stones. That would be considered unfair: one's *own* performance should be the only criterion.

Being straightforward is one thing, but expressing your real opinions another. In some languages people prefer voicing disapproval with terms or euphemisms such as 'not very good' or 'interesting'. In the case of the Dutch criticisms are barely concealed and certainly not expressed in euphemisms: good is good, bad is bad. This direct manner of expression can shock people who are not used to it. It is usually the first thing that crops up when I ask my target group here for their observations on the Dutch, quite irrespective of which country they come from. An observer from Australia: *'They make you feel that your choice of paint colour is stupid.'* And one from Britain: *'British people will not say what they think, except to very good friends. Here in Holland it may happen that someone asks you: why is your hair so long, why do you wear that tie with that shirt? I wouldn't be surprised if they told me: what an awful tie you're wearing! We British always worry whether we are doing the right thing, whether we are behaving properly. Dutchmen don't.'* No, they don't. In fact, they rather prefer honest criticism to flattering compliments.

Context   A better understanding of this explicit criticism requires some explanation of the structure of society and the Dutch way of making decisions. Given the socio-ideological pluriformity of the country there is rarely a majority opinion on any issue, and even if there is there will always be factions or individuals with a mind of their own. A BBC film aptly described Holland as *'a society of little boxes in a land of little squares'*.

No 'little box' has absolute power, so any decision, whether in companies, in Parliament, in the Town Hall or in a local volleyball club, involves debate and then compromise – water in the wine. If people don't clearly put forward their ideas, preferably backed up with sound arguments, they will not be reflected in the final decision. So opinions are expressed loudly and clearly, especially if they do not concern private emotional matters. And people do not give in until the final decision is made: *'They stick with their views.'* (Russia)

The Dutch are not afraid to make rather caustic comments to other groups in society, to those with other lifestyles. Sometimes this comes as a bit of a shock to foreigners, either because they are used to more political correctness, or because they thought that the Netherlands was a land of sweet tolerance to other people (see chapter 8). But people here are used to it, they do it mutually and since no one has a majority anyway, such comments are of no real consequence.

'Overleg'   Perhaps surprisingly, the term 'compromise' itself is not to be heard or read that often in everyday life. The word used for the (usually lengthy) process of reaching a compromise is *overleg*, a word which can be translated as 'deliberation'. This word suggests a time-consuming process and this is usually so;

on important issues overleg can take weeks, and every step taken in the process can produce new ideas for the parties involved and another reason for getting together again. This explains many of the infamous Dutch meetings about which quite a few expats grumble (see chapter 7). Then, when the inevitable compromise is finally reached and put down to paper, with everyone's carefully thought out arguments, an *overeenkomst* is reached: a word which – interestingly — not only means 'agreement', but also 'resemblance', 'similarity' or 'conformity'.

In the process of *overleg*, and in society as a whole, any fanaticism is frowned upon and even condemned. In companies and organisations managers fanatically defending a certain point of view must have both very strong arguments and a good deal of personal charisma – remember the Dutch tendency to use the words 'yes but'. In the Netherlands the ability to convince people is a better management tool than being good at power games!

Fairly typical of the somewhat detached manner of speech is the fact that in debates Dutch politicians use terms such as 'dismayed', 'alarmed' and 'perplexed' without their face indicating any of these strong feelings.

Critical attitudes and strong opinions, therefore, are clearly expressed, but usually in a rather non-emotional manner. Large parts of the Dutch population find a short and unequivocal word quite enough. For example the words *waardeloos* (worthless, useless, lousy) and *fout* (wrong, mistake) are often used, even among colleagues.

Rude words   Considerable numbers of people, and not only youngsters, use rude words (mostly three-letter words in Dutch) to express dislike or a negative opinion. And what often shocks native English speakers is that they sometimes use English four-letter words, which, being in a different language, don't sound quite so crude to the Dutch ear. Even when no rude words are used, Dutch opinions may come across very direct and strongly. Yet the speaker only feels (s)he is being honest with you. Part of the misunderstanding may also stem from the use of language – Dutch has several short words to 'soften' opinions *(maar, toch, even, een beetje)* but many people ignore them when translating into English. The result is that a comment or opinion sounds far blunter than the Dutch speaker intended it to be.

Rude words are rarely used in business, but critical attitudes do prevail. Your Dutch counterparts will inspect any proposal or performance in detail, ask questions, and give their straightforward, honest opinion. This leads people who are not used to such directness to call the Dutch 'opinionated', 'arrogant' and 'judgmental'. *'At college they often tell me: 'Gee, I didn't know Germans could be nice!''* (German student in Amsterdam). This remark might sound tactless and undiplomatic to non-Dutch people – but remember you are free, even expected, to make exactly the same type of remark. It is up to you to develop similar frankness. The Dutch might then describe you as being 'straight into the man' – and you should see it as a compliment. *'There is an obligation to have strong opinions'*, was the experience of a Polish participant on my course. *'It seems quite normal here to strongly disagree with your boss!'* (Britain)

As a matter of fact, after a while quite a few foreigners begin to appreciate Dutch directness. It may not be elegant, but at least *'you know where you stand'*. Not only criticism is voiced in direct ways, but also 'good advice'. This may not always be welcome, but the Dutch will feel it really is best for you. A language teacher from Trinidad: *'In my early days here, the most shocking thing to me was the directness. But after 18 years in Holland I know that when they say: 'Ann, run!', I'd better run.'* And from quite another culture: *'They are very helpful, and clear and direct in the answer they give you.'* (Germany)

More on Dutch English   Many people are quite impressed with the Dutch ability to speak English, but native speakers of English should realise that Dutch English is seldom 100% perfect. (A book on this issue introduced the term 'Dunglish'.) Linguistic misunderstandings may easily strengthen a native English speaker's impression that the Dutch are blunt or arrogant. A good example is the subtle difference in meaning between 'to propose' and 'to suggest'. A Dutch manager found his British colleagues irritated when innocently he used 'proposal' (a rather compelling hint) when he had actually meant 'suggestion' (a creative idea as good as any other one). Another example: in Amsterdam tram conductors often have to urge the public, entering at the back of the tram, to move forward to allow more passengers to board. As a courtesy to tourists they repeat themselves in 'English'. Now in Dutch one may omit the word 'please' without sounding too rude. But a harsh *'Move to the front, everybody!'* through the microphone may come as a bit of a shock to the non-Dutch.

So the Dutch speak their minds. Unlike people from, in particular, Asian cultures, loss of face is of little concern to many of them. *'Especially the directness of the Dutch was new to me, but I have got used to it by now. (…) As soon as I'm back in Japan, I switch to the norms of politeness that prevail there. There, if I don't agree to something, I don't say: 'No, you are wrong', as they do here.'* (Japan)

You ask a Dutch person for their opinion and you get it, clearly stated, no obscuring or disguising for the sake of politeness. The Dutch are programmed all their lives to deal with this, but many foreigners are shocked by this straightforwardness. They often perceive it as hostile and unfriendly. A German made an interesting point: *'Why do the Dutch keep saying 'heh?' after each statement?'* The answer may be that they are unconsciously gauging whether the person they are speaking to supports or opposes their opinion!

But here we come to a paradox: the Dutch will only treat you in this way if they take you seriously, if they feel you to be close enough, in the same 'little box' as they are. So, strange as it may sound, directness and criticism mean appreciation, belonging. They infer that you are one of us, that we accept you as more or less an equal.

If people don't feel this, they will critically observe you but not say much. In Dutch society, one should leave other 'little boxes' alone: live and let live. But we, here in our box, must strive for perfection and help each other to do so – how can anyone improve if they overlook their imperfections? So the Dutch tell each other what they think those imperfections are.

Self-criticism is also appreciated, as a group or an organisation but also at a strictly personal level. Probably a leftover of the Calvinistic guilt-ridden past, personal self-criticism seems to be waning in the current market-oriented mood, but at organisational levels it still goes on. Companies or departments organise brainstorming sessions to see what can be improved. If necessary, they will admit their mistakes publicly, albeit sometimes reluctantly. In the political world, there have been soul-searching parliamentary debates on what went wrong in incidents such as the Amsterdam plane crash of 1992 and the Dutch peacekeepers' involvement in the 1995 Srebrenica drama in Bosnia. As I write this, critical debate on the recent Enschede fireworks explosion is under way. Just about all the people involved must describe their doings in detail, 'with bare buttocks', as the Dutch say, and the various authorities shouldn't 'keep anything under their hat', in other words: hidden from the public.

At least some foreigners appreciate the critical stance of the Dutch, like this Nigerian: *'I appreciate the critical attitude of Dutch society. I like the way the media tackle touchy subjects, how they sometimes attack one another and how the authorities are open to the public. That is a good element in democracy.'*

Tell me what's wrong! In Dutch culture imperfections are a challenge, something that must be overcome by stubborn hard work: it *must* be perfect! An observer from Iceland: *'Dutch people are nice, but they criticise other people too often and too readily. Even when they discuss a match they won, they will constantly talk about the five minutes that things went a bit wrong. I don't know whether this is because they all know how to do things better, or because they just want to fuss.'*

The Dutch will analyse anything new. The good aspects are quickly taken for granted: perfect? OK, no longer interesting, let's go on looking for <u>im</u>perfections. These will be pointed out immediately and discussed: *'When you go to a concert or a theatre here, immediately afterwards everything is analysed, verbally cut to pieces.'* (Ireland)

Now you should not think criticism is always given in such a serious way, it can also be wrapped up in jokes, irony or sarcasm. Self-mockery and self-irony are also greatly appreciated, as a humorous kind of self-criticism. Projecting yourself small, making your performance relative is in line with the issue of equality, helps to make great achievement more palatable to the Dutch. The Dutch verb *'relativeren'* is often used. It means making things relative, seeing them in their proper perspective, not only in black and white. One might even see this as the verbal expression of the Dutch need for egalitarianism: avoid extremes, try to find the middle ground. This becomes particularly evident when a Dutch person receives a compliment. In line with the widespread critical attitude, compliments are not easily extended, since perfection is distrusted. In fact, too many compliments tend to make people uneasy and even if they are not met with disbelief, the receiver will usually wave them side, or self-mockingly 'make them relative'. In most cases *'prima'* (fine) will do. Superlatives like 'terrific', 'great' and the like are met with some suspicion and should be reserved for very special occasions only. A business woman from Hungary dryly observed: *'Good news is not welcomed here.'*

Perfection is merely duty, working on imperfections is one's real task in life. So tell us what's still wrong, please. The Icelander went on: *'They need to have a problem. If they don't have one, they'll look for one, because with a problem you can discuss: 'How are we going to solve it?''*

Task-oriented and serious *'In the short time I have been here what I have learned about the Dutch is that they are very straight, very much to the point and are always asking 'Why?'. The other thing is that they are eager to share their ideas, their brainpower, their thoughts.'* (Director of a large American company)

'You can tell the Dutch they are wrong, but you have to come with arguments <u>why</u> you think so. They are all professionals, but they're also careful. Give them your opinion and perhaps it may take six months, but they will come back on it by e-mail.' (Russian businessman)

The Dutch are task-oriented. What matters is that the product, the performance, is improved. Managers, as well as most of the other personnel, feel involved in their job and their company, so whatever changes are proposed they want to know why, what is your argumentation for this? They will ask critical questions, think it over, give direct feedback and go on discussing it until an agreement is reached between all the parties involved. On the other hand, when dealing with people from other countries this may not always be so easy to do: *'They are not so direct when they have to say 'no'.'* (Taiwan)

In the strive for perfection, the product, or if need be, the whole organisation, is verbally dismantled into its smallest components. Anything faulty is discussed, taken out and replaced by a better version, and then it's all reassembled. New, closer to perfection. Companies, ministries, organisations are restructured all the time, roads are under constant repair, houses are redecorated, office furniture is changed, computer systems updated, new rules are made. ('Change management' consultancy and training programmes for both managers and employees often accompany such reorganisations. The Dutch management-training sector is well developed and thriving.) And then when things are improved, let's not spend too much time on congratulating ourselves but get back to work, there is more to do. Quite a bit of time may be lost on this re-organising, but that seems to only bother foreigners: *'They question the why but not the what.'* (Britain)

This may all sound rather gloomy. But although the Dutch are serious this doesn't depress them, it's a challenge. Colleagues who have just critically discussed their common performance may go and have a pint together (but just one, see chapter 10). Discussion may go on at the bar and no-one is offended. Although the Dutch may not show it they quite enjoy this working on improvement. They talk about it, long and thoroughly, even intensely, but rarely with dramatic gestures or in very loud voices (remember: *'milk in their veins?'*). Such dramatic behaviour would undermine the speaker's point of view rather than strengthen it. Not too many emotions, please, and no superlatives. *'Sometimes the Dutch get on my nerves, their mentality is so different from mine. They are very reliable but terribly serious, so down to earth and cold. They observe life with their brains; everything goes according to the rules. I miss the Czech openness and spontaneity, the gaiety. Dancing and singing doesn't come easy to Dutchmen.'* (Czech Republic)

Organised *dancing and singing*   Maybe the Dutch are a little shy and uncertain because, in spite of the Czech comment, many Dutch people *do* dance and sing. It's just that they need a good excuse, a reason, and unless they are in the shower they don't like doing it alone. There are some 20,000 choirs in the Netherlands and there are many vocal festivals, choral singing competitions and even mass choirs and many a song is sung during football matches. As for dancing, every town has its discos, dance parties and dancing schools. But the Czech is right in the sense that all this is not spontaneous; virtually all of it is organised. People singing on the tram or dancing in the street will certainly receive curious looks or even frowns. Street musicians require licences from the local police. So spontaneity is not really appreciated. Only in weekend evenings – when, as everyone knows, quite a lot of alcohol has been drunk and people feel they have a good excuse – one might come across crowds of people singing and dancing.

So dancing and singing, or other expressions of emotion, don't come easy to the Dutch, certainly not in working hours. In public, most of the time, they come across as serious, looking earnest and concentrated, joking and smiling only occasionally. In Asia, a vague smile seems to be the average socially acceptable expression; Americans frequently burst into big smiles, while Latins have no problem in touching each other. But in Holland a stern look, a hushed voice and restrained movements are the norm, in public at least. Fulfilling your task, working hard and with concentration, even when it's at a hobby.

With a well-developed sense of duty and responsibility (and computers and machines to help them), the Dutch are approaching the highest productivity per hour worked in the world. Luckily for them they have long (paid) holidays. *'The Dutch are serious and they take everything seriously. You must be careful with jokes; they may easily get it wrong. This serious attitude is good for business, Dutch people are good at that.'* (Nigeria). And: *'In my experience, the Dutch are not capable of not taking things seriously, no matter what you say.'* (British philosopher Roger Scruton on Dutch TV).

But everything is relative – a Finnish friend once described the Dutch to me as *'real southerners"*! In spite of all their seriousness, the Dutch are apparently quite happy. For several years they have scored very highly in a Europe-wide survey on contentment with life. A Tanzanian commented: *'I like the way they smile here'*. Consistent with the directness issue, you can be sure that *when* they smile, they mean it! To my relief, a young Ukrainian management trainee said, after working for one month in a Dutch company: *'You really can learn a lot from the Dutch people. They are unique in questions of co-operation, timing, humour at work and work organisation. (....) You meet a lot of nice people here.'*

Occasionally you will even see Dutch people being very enthusiastic ('going out of their roof', is the literal translation of a contemporary Dutch expression for this). That used to be only in private, in the company of friends or relatives. In public, it always took a 'valid' reason, ranging from football matches through Queen's Day to stag nights, and almost certainly a drink or two (or ten).[1] The result is not always pleasant to witness. Like me, you'll probably prefer to avoid football stadiums and their environs on match days!

Back at work, what counts is that the product is improved, the target reached. The constant striving for perfection is a (subconscious) part of Dutch upbringing. Most people deal with criticism and the lack of compliments in a somewhat detached manner: this here is me and that over there is what I do, so feel free to shoot.

Conflicts and decision making   Sometimes, of course, people do become hurt or angry. If 'talking it over' no longer helps, there are various other calm solutions: the people involved can simply ignore each other, or if regular encounters are unavoidable, superiors can reorganise work to keep them to the absolute minimum. There is no need to get excited about it, let alone violent. The same applies on a more collective scale, the same applies. *'In other countries conflicts easily* *escalate. Here people stay calm. The company council, the trade unions and the company directors take decisions in relative harmony.'* (Switzerland)

Yes, this striving for harmony, for solving conflict by way of discussion, is at the basis of the 'polder model'. Labour disputes and strikes are not totally unknown in the Netherlands, but less time is lost to them than in most other European countries. Collective labour agreements often include no-strike agreements. If they don't, strikes may only take place – after serious negotiating has failed – by court permission. In this case the trade unions will support the strikers and pay their wages. 'Wildcat' strikes, unlawful and not backed by the unions, do take place occasionally, but as the strikers have no income they never last long. New negotiations are bound to follow. In fact, merely threatening to strike can sometimes be enough to bring a thaw to frozen negotiations. Angry strikers marching or waving protest banners are a rare phenomenon in the Netherlands. (When I recently ran into such a group in front of the headquarters of a large multinational company, I thought to myself: now that's old-fashioned! I later found out that the strikers were French...)

In business and in government the usual reaction to important and controversial problems is to form a 'working group', a 'committee', a 'commission of wise people' or some other forum in order to discuss the issue at hand and look for harmonious solutions. People on such committees are carefully chosen to represent various views on the issue involved. The conclusion is that solving conflicts or problems in Holland just takes a lot of talking, so please have your opinion ready, and state it, clearly!

'It's unbelievable how often the Dutch hold meetings. Where do they find the time? And yet they don't discuss very well, because people always want to be nice to each other.' (Germany)

Long discussions have always been part of Dutch culture. In the old days they were often religious in nature.[2] Nowadays they are concerned with politics, random violence, new legislation, anything, anywhere: over lunch, at parties, in pavement cafés, at campsites. And on television, of course. Compared to American talk shows, Dutch talk shows are – again – quite serious and lack glamour. During such a debate, on TV or elsewhere, one may see quite earnest faces, both among the speakers and the public. But at the same time such debate is rather fun to the Dutch, serious fun. It is like a game of chess, thoughtful and precise, everybody calmly waiting their turn and yet excited by the content of the discussion. Reflecting Holland's social pluriformity, widely differing points of view may, and will, be expressed, so it can take quite some time before any conclusion is reached. You will not be surprised by now to hear that Holland has many political parties and their debates take up much time, sometimes lasting into the wee small hours. *'I think the Dutch urge to have meetings comes from the need to avoid conflict and to take decisions in harmony. But I have learned to be alert. For hours and hours they talk in circles and then when you doze off, they suddenly take a decision in thirty seconds. And then it is irrevocable.'* (Britain)

Lengthy decision making may be threatening company meetings too, involving people at different levels. In recent years a speedier decision making process has come to be appreciated and stimulated, especially in 'fast' sectors like ITC. But in more traditional industry many non-Dutch people think it still takes far too long, as it did to another American observer some years ago: *'In the [Dutch] company where I work, I exclaimed: for heaven's sake, let's stop talking about it and DO something!'* But in spite of what the Dutch see as more efficient procedures, apparently not much has changed: on a very recent Dutch culture programme, participants coming from various other European countries wrote the following list of observations they had made so far on this subject: *'They talk too much'*, *'Consensus, long meetings'*, *'Too democratic?'*, *'Consensus is time-consuming'* and *'Each discussion is a real meeting with an appointment and a* kopje koffie' *(cup of coffee).*

There is a good side too, however, as expressed by this Frenchman: *'Yes, decision making in Holland takes an awfully long time, but everybody is heard in the process and once the decision is finally taken, all seem to recognise their point of view in it somehow, so they will implement it.'*

And that is exactly what counts: everyone consulted and involved, harmony safeguarded. This happens at all levels, including the way in which the government deals with private enterprise. The same Swiss quoted above, observed: *'The agreements that (Dutch) enterprise have made with the government are unique. In every other country environmental laws are dictated by the authorities, which then evokes resistance from the companies involved.'*

It would be a little too optimistic to think that such agreements are always met with general approval and enthusiasm, but all in all, yes, Holland is a country where things are talked over and compromise reached. This is essential for maintaining social harmony and getting people to work for the common cause. Compromise at all cost: if extra costs are needed to satisfy all parties (provided their arguments are sound), so be it. '*I was impressed with the Dutch culture oriented on co-operation and finding compromise which resulted in the Delta project and the wealth of the country as whole.*' (Ukrainian management trainee)

Compromise In the 1980s, a giant dam was constructed in the southwest of the country. People who put forward economic and ecological arguments for not building a dam at all were opposed by people wanting a permanent 'closed' dam to prevent a repetition of the disastrous floods of 1953. After long debate all parties won, but at much greater cost than had been foreseen. The compromise was an open construction that could be closed within half an hour. On the other hand, the idea of creating a very costly extension of Schiphol Airport in the North Sea, for ecological and safety reasons, was finally abandoned in 1999, after lengthy debate: it was considered to be too expensive and potentially damaging to the marine environment.

But usually social harmony and compromise between conflicting opinions are dearly bought in a nation of reputedly money-minded people.

After centuries of deep religiousness a measure of moralism has crept into Dutch criticism. Wagging the forefinger has become a recurring phenomenon: you are wrong, I am right. Although unpopular, this attitude is widespread, both within the country itself and – sometimes coming as shock – in international dealings, too. There are regular calls to boycott this or that country because of its bad environmental policy, its abuse of human rights, or anything else the Dutch public disapproves of. Governments abroad have received thousands of postcards from Dutch people protesting (in organised campaigns) against racist incidents, nuclear testing or whaling.

At official levels Dutch government functionaries have had the honour of being told by foreign hosts (behind the scenes, usually) that it would be better if they kept some of their opinions to themselves. Some painful incidents have occurred. At a conference on the international image of the Netherlands, a former (post-apartheid) South African ambassador said: '*The pointed Dutch finger is well known throughout the world. Sometimes this attitude must be applauded (...in the pursuit of human rights ideals...), but sometimes this judgmental attitude should be expressed more carefully.*'

Companies, too, can be accused of misdemeanours such as polluting the environment, investing in undemocratic countries, or using some dangerous, materials. In the past, demonstrations, boycotts and even violent protests followed. Nowadays, if an accident occurs during the production process, the company concerned will immediately publicise it and offer extensive apologies and promise to improve their production methods, rather than wait for the public storm to break. Such action is appreciated, and has the advantage of stifling much of the potential protest. (I cannot explain, by the way, the fact that unlike elsewhere in Europe genetic manipulation is scarcely a public issue in the Netherlands – not so far, at least).

In spite of the continuous struggle to achieve perfection there are still imperfections. Foreign expatriates complain about government bureaucracy, slow service, short banking and shopping hours (they are apparently unimpressed by the longer opening hours which have been in place since 1996), unclear procedures when plumbers and electricians come to their homes and poor facilities for working women (see chapter 10). The Dutch themselves may complain about all this and much more, plus the weather, of course. You may have to get used to welcoming phrases such as 'Terrible weather today, did you get very wet?', and to unexpected summer heat in buildings which are not air-conditioned. *'The Dutch have everything under control, except for the weather. So that becomes a topic of general conversation.'* (Nepal) But this should be seen as a national sport. A Dutchman with nothing to complain about would be a very unhappy person.

Backgrounds   We will now turn to some historical backgrounds to Dutch outspokenness. Directness is, of course, more than just a language thing; underneath it lies an attitude. Protestant religion, besides stressing one's duties to live a frugal and productive life, emphasises the importance of 'the Word'. From the beginning this led to taking the Bible quite literally, and to sharp distinctions between God and the devil, good and bad, right and wrong, us and them – in other words, to thinking in sharply dualistic categories. In the Calvinist society that much of the Netherlands was until the 1960s, emotions were restrained and spontaneity was frowned upon: singing was restricted to church services and birthday parties, and dancing was considered sinful.

Like other 'holy books', the Bible isn't always very clear and indeed can be quite paradoxical, and this has led to a multitude of interpretations from individual believers and various denominations. 'A nation of church ministers', as the Dutch themselves say. Even today it is still normal in many a Calvinist household to privately discuss and judge the sermon after attending a church service.

Although for centuries the Dutch Reformed church was the major church, there were always internal and external debates and struggles going on and these often led to break-away denominations – from the early 1600s up to as recently as 1944. Over the years, all kinds of religious interpretations were debated, sometimes bitterly. In trying to make their point debaters put forward what they hoped were well-considered arguments, while voicing 'rational' and very direct, moralising criticism of other parties' points of view. In my view, the roots of Dutch directness and judgmental attitudes lie in these everlasting religious debates.

There is more to it than just religious pluriformity and outspoken-ness. Dutch directness also springs from great self-confidence and – again – the relatively low hierarchy. For over 200 years, until the changes inspired by the French Revolution in 1795, the country was a federal republic. It had emerged out of the 16th-century uprising against Spanish rule. Under the banner of Protestantism, which gave them support from the rank and file, local nobles and merchants aspired to political and economic autonomy from foreign rule, and won. In other words the Dutch republic was a kind of 'self-made' country. People felt their leaders had been appointed by they themselves, unlike the absolute monarchs who ruled in neighbouring countries. Since adherence to strict Calvinism coincided with great prosperity the Dutch felt they were under divine protection. Other countries' admiration of the republic's modern institutions con-tributed to a sense of moral superiority, shared by all.

The republic was pluriform from the start; no group could really impose its will. Be it interpretations of the Bible, colonial policy or new laws and taxes, everything was discussed and differing views had to be accommodated somehow: compromise. A number of more authoritar-ian periods ended in riots and upheaval. Authority was all right as long as the public felt it to be ordained by God, then they obeyed.

The most recent large-scale questioning of authority occurred in 1966, when general dissatisfaction among the younger generation brought down university deans and burgomasters. Amsterdam, addicted to the drug of freedom, played the leading role. With one or two exceptions, these social changes happened fairly peacefully, but only after very long discussions indeed. There was a new element however – a good deal of mockery and laughter. This was the ideology of the youth movement: playfulness, fantasy, down with all those serious and solemn autocrats. This generation had been brought up with the funny books by children's author Annie M. G. Schmidt and the TV shows they inspired. A former schoolteacher, she advocated a mild 'naughtiness' in children, autonomy from adults, who pretend to be stern and ever-strict but are hypocritical and childish themselves. The books of this beloved, kind, perfect grandmother-figure have been published in translation world-wide, but for those who do not know her work, perhaps the title of a post-mortem collection of her writings says enough: *'Never do as your mother tells you!'*…

More humour has come into Dutch public culture since the 1960s. Irony, satire and self-mockery became part of many political campaigns and social movements, even of advertising, and this is appreciated by the public. A very popular art-form in Holland is *cabaret*: a kind of one-(wo)man show with a mixture of laughter at the pomposity of the 'authorities', bits of philosophy, a song here and there, and lots of mockery at the Dutch themselves, including the audience. The rather ironic comments on other social groups that we mentioned above, also appear in this art form. At times, cabaretiers explore the limits of taboos and political correctness by exposing hypocrisy on sensitive issues like racism, discrimination and religion. Over the years, this has caused several minor scandals, with some people writing critical letters to the papers and others defending whatever stance had been taken. But once again, remember that criticism is appreciation in disguise!

Inspired by such entertainment, Dutch television advertisements also tend to use humour and mild social criticism, several of them winning awards at international festivals. To summarise: the honesty and effectiveness of criticism and outspokenness is considered far more important than the status of either the speaker or the person commented upon. As long as basic standards of common decency are respected, anything goes – as long as it is likely to lead to improvement. Other people's right to think in their own way should be respected, harmony should be maintained. But Dutch standards in this field may still surprise people from other countries!

1. Over recent years, several fatal incidents of alcohol-related 'random violence' have caused upheaval in Dutch society.
2. In the 1600s, half of all the books published in Holland – and they were many – dealt with religion and theological debate!

Chapter 6

PRAGMATIC AND MONEY-MINDED

'Fried air'
(Dutch slang expression for pompous talk or useless objects)

'Dutch disaster relief is very well-organised and efficient', observed a Belgian news reporter a few hours after the tragic Enschede fireworks explosion in May 2000. It's fairly typical of the Dutch: there may be a great deal of emotion and political uncertainties involved, but first let's do what needs to be done, let's remain practical.[1] The Dutch are pragmatic people, with a highly developed sense of realism in combination with 'down to earth-ness'.

Dutch art also reflects this attitude. In the 17th century artists such as Rembrandt and Vermeer painted common people engaged in their simple everyday activities, and in the 19th century Van Gogh painted poor peasants. In the 20th century Mondriaan became famous for his colourful grid-patterns, which could be interpreted as abstractions of Holland's man-made, rational landscapes with flower bulbs and canals. The Dutch art-scene has also produced a number of superrealist painters who do not leave out a single leaf of a tree, or one feather of a bird. In literature, too, the Dutch seem to have more of a turn for prose than for poetry, and their prose is usually realistic, expressing everyday concerns, rather than fantasy. In recent years, 'confession literature' has become quite popular. As its name suggests, this type of literature describes true but mostly unspectacular events in the author's life, often in great detail.

A Russian translator has a poetic theory about it: *'Dutch people have to consider every step they take, otherwise they run into a wall, a fence, a corner. They are forced to be concrete, and they actually like the concreteness produced by their lack of space. But at the same time they want to break out. Look at all those canals in Holland, they fade away into endlessness.'*

Indeed, the Dutch like concreteness, and they are good at it. In line with the inclination to task-orientation, described in chapter 5, they tend to focus on content and purpose. While at work the problem, or the issue itself, is more interesting than the people involved. No nonsense, just act normal and be useful. Practical aspects, such as time schedules, prices, and other concrete conditions are dealt with in great detail verbally, on paper and in action. In society in general, outside the immediate circle of one's family and friends, this rather functional approach to other people, rational and unemotional, prevails. This is especially striking to people from cultures where this brain/heart-separation is not so strong. This may lead the Dutch to overlook 'external' aspects such as personal contact, prestigious appearance, ceremony and circumstance.

They tend to get down to business without allowing much time to get to know their counterparts. Within minutes they begin to focus on the purpose of the meeting, to discuss the qualities of the product involved, the details of the transaction. Sometimes even fellow Dutch people find this approach too hasty. Literally translated, the expression used for such impatient behaviour is 'invading the house with the door' – battering the door down rather than wasting time looking for your keys! Yet it is done all the time, certainly among people working together every day in an office. This approach is not consciously impolite, but because people can be so task-oriented they just forget the last time they saw you was yesterday: *'Hey, about that proposal you mentioned…'*. In business encounters of all kinds the Dutch want to get 'past the post' as quickly as possible. Small wonder, then, that after the initial personal contact or round of negotiation, further steps may well be made by telephone or through faxes and e-mails.

To business partners from more relationship-oriented cultures this approach can appear to be impatient and unsophisticated, maybe coming on top of irritation about Dutch directness: *'The Dutch have a trading mentality: they want to see results immediately.'* (Pakistan). And: *'Dutch people have too much of a business mentality.'* (Iran)

People from faster moving societies don't always agree: *'They are trying to be efficient but things take forever.'* (Great Britain), but this again referred to internal decision making in a company. Whether or not they are impatient or slow, the Dutch make up for these faults by being trustworthy and punctual in the subsequent follow-up. In a 1997 survey for a congress on the national image abroad[2], Dutch respondents from various sectors of society congratulated themselves by naming 'trustworthiness' as their main positive achievement. (Being pragmatic and critical, of course, the congress then devoted most of its time to discussing the more negative points, and what to do about them.)

In their leisure time the Dutch are quite fond of philosophising but during work they do not appreciate vagueness, castles in the air, talk that is not down to earth. Ideas and activities are all right as long as they lead to practical, measurable effects. An Amsterdam-based American businesswoman boiled it all down with the term '*Newtonian*': analytical, rational, calculating, unambiguous, 'brainy'. It implies figures and facts, measures and weights, statistics and computing, calculating probability and estimating outcome. Behind it lies an appreciation of a rather strict separation of emotions and rationality. The Dutch (positive!) word used for this attitude is '*nuchter*', meaning 'matter-of-fact' but also: sober, without alcohol....

Later on we will see that there are a lot of '*nuchter*' people in Holland, in every corner of society. But all this rationality obviously has its drawbacks, too. A Dutch business consultant who worked in the US comments: *'The Dutch carefulness has its advantages but also its disadvantages. It goes at the cost of speed and the willingness to experiment. I am convinced we could make more of it if we let ourselves be guided more by passion and intuition rather than this rationality again and again.'* But such a change of attitude is hard to achieve, and in the reality of Dutch present-day 'society of little boxes', this is not yet quite the case.

Achieved status   Rationality and pragmatism have other effects, too. In more relationship-oriented cultures business people may like to position themselves by hinting at their good education, their prestigious family backgrounds, their power as a boss, their good relations with politicians. None of this appeals very much to the Dutch; it makes them feel uneasy. They tend to find such positioning and posturing irrelevant and a waste of time, maybe even pompous or cocky. The chances are it will weaken your image rather than strengthen it. It is the *product* they are interested in, the transaction, the successful business deal. If your product is good and the price is right they'll be happy to trade with you.

In Dutch business culture one's own performance is the criterion that counts, not any assets one might have inherited. Things may be different in private life, but at work one's status should be 'achieved' rather than 'acquired'. Using family backgrounds, friends in high places or other forms of patronage to make your way to the top is disapprovingly called 'using a wheelbarrow'. This is not always easily distinguished from networking, but one effect is that rich people in Holland often keep their children on rather tight budgets when they are studying. In this way they are not spoilt, but have to fight for themselves and so grow strong. The aristocracy – recognisable to the

Dutch public from their long, several-barrelled, family names – usually choose to shorten their name in public so that they do not stand out.

In business encounters with the Dutch it is therefore advisable to stick close to the current concern. Do not dwell on subjects such as history, philosophy, or the wonderful architecture of the city. A short appreciative remark about the city or the country is more than sufficient. And don't spend more than the absolute minimum amount of time on your personal background and mention any prestigious contacts outside business only casually. Of course most Dutch people are polite enough to go along for a while, but they will probably be wondering why you are bringing all this up: you're here on business, aren't you?

So, within minutes of beginning your meeting show your product, talk of its qualities, stress its usefulness for the customer, bring out the prospectuses, ask the other party's specific needs, show them how you can meet these, answer their questions and mention the price . Your Dutch counterpart will not say it out loud, but will probably be thinking: 'This is the right person to deal with – clear and direct, coming to the point!' And don't be surprised or dismayed by critical questions, of course: remember that to the Dutch nothing can ever be perfect!

Now don't think the Dutch shrink from philosophical discussion, debate or having fun. They like these things, but it is felt that they belong outside business hours, afterwards, at the golf club, at a company reception, in a break at a management-training programme. 'Business comes before the girlfriend', the expression goes. *'I find the Dutch quite focussed.'* (Ireland)

Status and hierarchy are also easily considered rather irrelevant 'girl friends'. Visiting factories of a Dutch company in various tropical countries I was told how local workers were surprised to see their Dutch managers rolling up their sleeves when a machine broke down. Not afraid of getting their hands dirty hands or oil stains on their clothes, they did the job that needed doing, rather than losing precious time by getting in the person whose job this really was. Certainly in an emergency: be equal, be pragmatic!

Waste not…! An important part of the pragmatic approach to business is, of course, money. The Dutch proverbially take the Scots as examples of tightness with money, but the Scots, and people from many other countries, point to the Dutch as classic examples of stinginess. English language has the expression 'going Dutch', meaning splitting the bill and paying for oneself, while Belgians tell quite a few jokes about the tight-fisted Dutch. For a change, the following quotations are from other perspectives: *'It is striking how there's always a price tag attached here. In Holland people immediately ask what things cost. Whether it is the shortage of prison cells, a new railway line or an UN-building in The Hague: how much will it cost? That is a kind of stinginess you also meet on a small scale.'* (Germany) And: *'Sometimes I find the Dutch very, very mean. I sometimes feel they're only thinking of money and how to save it.'* (Norway) Visitors from various countries comment with dismay on the fact that in department stores and railway stations they have to pay for using the toilet. My defence that at least those toilets are kept clean, doesn't seem to impress them. (Almost with relief I recently noticed that one often needs to pay for this in Germany and Switzerland, too...)

Company hospitality   The Dutch can be pragmatic to the point of being rude. Let me give the following illustration. In 1999, I worked with Belgian people whose Brussels branch office was in the process of being merged with the Dutch branch office to form the common Benelux-office of their American-owned firm. They had arranged accommodation in a rather splendid city centre hotel for my colleague and me. When we thanked them for this, they told us the following: *'We always arrange that hotel for guests, also for our Dutch colleagues when they come here, and they appreciate it very much. But when we come to their out-of-town office in Holland, they only arrange for us to stay at this nearby simple motel....'* I'm not sure if I succeeded in convincing these Belgians that this had perhaps more to do with pragmatism than with stinginess...

It is true that the Dutch are money-minded. Seven centuries of trading must have penetrated the national psyche. Selling and buying, negotiating, getting a better price represent fun to the Dutch, very serious fun. When I asked a group of expats what they thought was the most striking aspect of the Dutch, one German immediately said: *'business attitudes'*.... Places like auctions, flea markets and second hand shops are popular for satisfying this need. Some nations may challenge fortune by gambling, most Dutch people prefer safeguarding the future by steady saving and by chasing bargains. In spite of growing consumerism, saving is still widely popular, always has been. The large Dutch banking sector rests on capital accumulated in the past by frugal citizens and merchants. In the 17th century, Amsterdam was one of Europe's main financial centres, and it still is fourth, exceeded only by London, Paris and Frankfurt. Given the low interest rates in recent years, people now prefer to invest their money in real estate, art, and the stock market. Some invest in the high-risk ventures in the 'New Economy' while others are tempted by rather dubious ostrich farms. Other people prefer low-profit but environmentally friendly enterprises such as teak plantations (replacing forest clearance) or idealistic banks giving loans to poor farmers in developing countries. Yet most people still choose the old, solid funds represented on the Amsterdam Stock Exchange, the world's oldest! The total amount of Dutch savings and investments runs into almost incomprehensibly large figures. In spite of the great wealth, old habits die hard: the Central bank of the Netherlands calculated that the Dutch still save more of every rise of income than Britons and Americans.

In recent years, some special problems have arisen in this field, luxury problems: organisations such as charities, some public bodies such as schools – and even an entire province were found to have so much surplus money that they had started playing the stock market rather than accepting the low interest offered by the banks. Most people did not approve. The government ordered the province to reverse this policy, while parents and contributors to charity also enforced other approaches.

Government economising   The Dutch state has been vigorously economising on all kinds of activities ever since the 1970s, wanting to prove to tax-payers it spends every guilder wisely. Although with present-day budget surpluses there is less need to economise, expenditure must still be accounted for. The 'General Chamber of Calculations' is an important government body in this matter, and after the presentation of new government policy in September the ministries must account for their actions and financial policies.

Sometimes the money-snake may bite its own tail. In August 2000, a devastating report indicated that due to years of economising on academic studies the Dutch health care system, once one of the best in the world, is now lagging behind due to a serious shortage of doctors and specialists. This, together with the shortage of nursing staff, means that there are now long waiting lists for operations and special treatments. In order to find nursing personnel, health care campaigns with the catchy but somewhat desperate slogan: 'health care, the *real* work!' The technical standards of Dutch health care are still excellent still, but the waiting list problem, unknown in surrounding countries, is so serious that it has started to reduce older people's life expectancy. The immediate and rather predictable ministerial reaction was: more money! In 2001, over 3 billion guilders allocated for pay raises and better working conditions in the health sector should solve most of the problems.

Penny wise   The Dutch don't only save money in bank accounts or through share portfolios, they also do it in small ways. When you shop in a Dutch supermarket the cashier will ask you almost ritually: 'Do you have a bonus card? Do you save air miles, stamps?' Trying to bind increasingly 'opportunistic' and 'less loyal' younger customers to their organisation with discounts and 'air miles' is a popular ploy of supermarkets, department stores and gas stations these days. But the traditional saving stamp is also still around: the older generations used to cut out and save small gift coupons from products such as our most famous brand of coffee, and some people still do so.

In both cases, the motivation is the same – feel you are being a smart consumer by saving money! Many people do it, it is almost a national hobby. (Apparently we're not the only ones however: *'The Dutch love freebies, like us Indians'*, someone said on my course. And someone from Bulgaria joked: *'We also have scrooges, but only in the town of Gabrovo.'*)

Be it small scale in private life or large scale in the world of business, the Dutch like to bargain. It's a sport, one expects the opponent to be equally cunning, and one is proud when one wins. Again, the task at hand is the whole purpose, hurt feelings are only side-effects. An old complaint about the Dutch, made by an English observer who apparently struck bad luck both at work and in private life:
'In love and in commerce, the fault of the Dutch
is giving too little and asking too much.'

Leaving the matter of love to your private investigation, we will concentrate on the issue of commerce. Although the Dutch may not exactly take this couplet as a compliment, they'll probably think: too bad for him, he should have bargained better! ING bank (and with it, quite a few Dutch newspaper readers) was very proud when it cunningly bought the British Barings bank for a symbolic one pound at the moment it was virtually bankrupt Similar low-cost acquisitions – although not quite that low – have taken place more recently.

One doesn't speak of a good selling price of course – like salaries, one's profits are a well-kept secret – but a good buying price is often mentioned as an extra asset to the purchase, not only in business but also privately. Any large expense is carefully considered beforehand, in government, in business, in the family. So in the unlikely event that your price is quickly accepted, you are surely selling too cheaply!

Following the biblical advice on 'using one's talents', Calvinism taught that profits should not lead to frivolous enjoyment. Loans and credits for such purposes were also frowned upon (let alone gambling of any kind!), one should save, and only spend what has already been earned by virtuous hard work. Do not borrow money and always pay cash, was the message, and to a large degree it still is: obtaining money from cash points is more widely popular than using cheques or credit cards, much to the dislike of some expatriates. The banks stimulate this, since it costs them less. (It costs them even less when people do all their banking digitally because it saves a lot of paper-work, so they give away CD-ROMs 'free', as a 'service'.) This attitude also plays a role in e-commerce, because so far this has not become particularly popular: only 31% of the population has ever bought something through Internet, in spite of the high degree of computeri-sation in households. The Dutch don't trust e-commerce very much: wondering whether it is safe to pay electronically by credit card, and if the product will be all that they say it is.

Possibly this cash-orientation is also a consequence of trading worldwide in times long gone in regions outside any banking net-work, which stimulated immediate payment in cash or kind.

Yet there are paradoxes, even when it comes to money. In spite of its reputation, this nation that eagerly accumulates money and saves it, spends it just as easily. It s expenditure on international schemes such as development co-operation, relief funds, UN peace missions, supporting ecological projects world-wide, and so on, represents one of the highest percentages of gross national product in the world. Privately, too, the Dutch raise large sums of money in televised actions for all kinds of charities. Local or international charitable organisations distribute easy-to-fill-out cheques, and raise so much money that it became public knowledge that, lacking suitable projects, some of them invested it in the stock exchange. In 1998 and '99, within twelve months, tens of millions of guilders were collected for victims of the hurricane in Nicaragua, for the Kosovo refugees and again for victims of the Turkish earthquake. (It should be added that over a certain amount such gifts are tax-deductible.) Street collections usually raise quite a bit of money. *'Yep, the people in general and the companies are tight with money. But of course, there are exceptions to every rule – some of my colleagues and at least one friend are far more generous than anyone I've ever met.'* (USA)

A lady from Mauritius, having lived in Holland for some twenty years, told me: *'I have come to the conclusion that the Dutch are not stingy after all. They just hate to waste anything.'* Wasting, that is the keyword. In Dutch culture, traditionally, one did not spend for enjoyment, one saved or re-invested. Even nowadays, if the Dutch find an expense to be necessary, useful, well worthwhile, then they spend. If they find it to be a luxury, extravagant, superfluous, then they don't. This is reflected in advertising, where the low price is often more strongly stressed than aspects like quality, technical specifications, status and usefulness. Only in ads aimed at the top levels of the market is the price argument less prominent.

Money is not the sole incentive   As throughout the whole world, money and other material perks are important motivations for Dutch managers and employees alike. Companies tempt the much-wanted young professionals by offering a car, fitness facilities at work, a laundry service, or other conveniences meant to balance the requirements of the job. But quite a few job-hoppers, albeit in a minority, try to find a working environment that offers more than just good material conditions. They go for non-material things: fulfilment, self-development, a sense of usefulness to society, or even to the world. Some value these things more than a high salary. Besides offering fringe benefits such as sabbaticals, childcare facilities and the like, companies also need to think harder about what distinguishes them from their competitors: what can they offer as extra motivation? What is their mission in the world? Some consultants earn their living advising on these matters. I tend to see this development as a substitute for old-time religiousness, as the modern expression of the old struggle between mundane and spiritual values.

Of course, with the general prosperity and relaxation of moral attitudes since the 1960s spending has become easier for the Dutch and the nation is shopping and consuming like never before. (Nowadays, with low interest rates, Dutch households are starting to take out more loans for immediate consumption, but even now the average debt of some 2000 euros is very low when put into an international perspective). The Dutch are still great savers. The extensive and internationally successful Dutch banking and finance sector is based on very large amounts of money safely tucked away in bank accounts, in shares and in property.

In many other ways the Dutch 'keep an apple for thirst', as they say. The government workers' pension fund (ABP), now privatised, is one of the largest investment funds in the world, quite disproportionate to the country's population. Some company pension funds are so wealthy that employees no longer pay contributions, some have even paid money back to the company (the unions demand that workers, past and present, should also benefit).

The Netherlands being a rich country, what is the point of this money-mindedness, one might wonder. The expression 'going Dutch' and the rhyme quoted above (both British in origin) are some 300 years old. This trait is deeply rooted in the Dutch character and I cannot help thinking that it can be traced back to Calvinist sobriety and thrift. This also manifests itself in the attention paid to the environment – don't waste! Besides national policies on this issue, most individual households happily contribute by separating paper, glass and organic waste, stimulated by TV and radio spots saying: 'a cleaner environment starts with yourself'. Over 90% of all glass and paper is recycled these days and the recycling industry has grown tremendously. But not everybody is concerned, people still litter the streets and dump rubbish in areas of natural beauty. All in all, there is quite a bit of both moralism and hypocrisy in the general concern for the environment.

Consuming less   The present level of wealth and consumption is not to everyone's liking. Some people in Holland consciously refuse to live conspicuous lifestyles. For environmental reasons, in solidarity with the poor in the Third World, as a protest against 'over-consumption', or as a combination of these, such people opt for less income and a simple life. A few abandon their often well-paid careers, seeking a way to make what they see as a more useful contribution to society. They may work in health care, education or social work, either part-time or as a volunteer. One couple proudly calling themselves the 'Misers' began to publish a 'non-glossy lifestyle magazine' with tips and hints on how to lead a simple but healthy and pleasant life, on recycling, vegetarian cooking, do-it-yourself, how to adjust to a sober lifestyle, how to react to hostility from the outside world, and so on.

The largely practical attitudes of the Dutch are in line with their sense of equality and their general directness in conversation. The religiously inspired sobriety of yesteryear is becoming a thing of the past, times have changed and continue to change. Nonetheless there are still a number of somewhat ascetic aspects to Dutch culture, in spite of all the cafés, restaurants, amusement parks and partying.

Food   Take food, for instance. *'You Dutch don't find food interesting, for us Italians it is much more important. Put five or six Italians together – serious business people, good friends, whatever – and in no time they will be discussing food. Not the Dutch, they have other ways of enjoying themselves.'* (Italy). I am tempted to say: when in Rome....

Indeed, food is a topic that relatively few Dutch people bother to discuss. In a way food was (and in some circles still is) seen simply as the fuel necessary to keep one fit to perform one's function – so there isn't really that much to talk about. But in their own defence the Dutch may point out that they have a long life expectancy, generally enjoy good health and, on average, are one of the world's tallest nations. So their food and their eating habits can't be all that bad! In recent years, however, the Dutch have started to appreciate good food more, and several Dutch restaurants have been awarded the famous Michelin stars (but none of them the maximum number). Nonetheless, foreigners living here are not impressed. Based on observations in company canteens, they conclude – wrongly – that deep-fried high-cholesterol snacks are 'traditional Dutch food'.

Let's take a look at traditional Dutch eating habits. Dutch dinners are usually brief and simple and eaten at around 6.30 PM. Generally speaking, fresh ingredients are used, although nowadays a wide variety of ready-made meals is available in every supermarket. The meal usually starts with soup (most visitors are enthusiastic about Dutch soups!) and this is followed by a small portion of meat with potatoes (boiled, fried or mashed) and one type of vegetable, and a simple dairy-based dessert.

If there are no guests or visitors, lunch at work will most likely be taken in the company canteen, at home at the kitchen table. *'Lunch here is like a second breakfast'*, some people comment on the generally sober meal which basically consists of different sorts of bread, thinly sliced meats and cheese, and milk. As extras, a bowl of soup, a hot snack, a salad or a piece of fruit may be eaten.

In such canteens one can observe people from all levels of the company (though not usually at the same table) eating a quick, simple lunch, maybe buying soup or a hot snack to supplement sandwiches brought from home. There's always work waiting, so there's no time for a long leisurely meal. Working lunches consumed during meetings are even more Spartan: *'Dutch lunches during meetings are soft bread and milk.'* Long meals are a waste of time, so it's hardly a surprise to learn that Dutch business people have the shortest lunch breaks in Europe! And many people – not just schoolchildren, but people in business, banking and government, too – can be seen carrying their lunch boxes from home. This is in line with the Dutch character: practical, cheap and ignoring hierarchy or status. One last complaint: *'There are no pub visits here during lunchtime.'* No, and definitely not for alcohol.

All the same, you mustn't think the Dutch are unable to enjoy good food, or that their taste buds are inferior to other people's. Every city has a variety of restaurants and most of them will be full at the right time of day. At home, too, many Dutch people take pleasure in good cooking and enjoy preparing extensive dinners. Yet it is still uncommon for most people, especially outside the Randstad, to have dinner in town more than perhaps once a week, or to prepare a four-course meal at home. Family life and evening obligations just don't make this an option, as we will see later on.

Since the 1960s eating out is no longer exceptional, but given the sober nature of their own cuisine the Dutch prefer more exotic food. In fact, 'Dutch' restaurants are a rarity! Cuisines from the four corners of the world can be sampled in all the larger cities and when people are invited round for dinner, the chances are a foreign recipe will be chosen rather than a Dutch one. Nowadays supermarkets not only sell now traditional Indonesian ingredients, but Thai, Indian, Mexican and many, many others. Large numbers of Turks and Moroccans live in the Netherlands and food from these countries is also widely available, often in specialist shops.

If your Dutch business partner does take you out for dinner, be pre-pared: *'They kept us sitting at the table all evening, while we were still jet-lagged!'* (USA). In the European tradition 'eating out' is an event that can go on until very late at night and it is usually accompanied by 'meaningful conversation'. Some other complaints I hear regularly: *'There is only mineral water available in restaurants, for which they charge you.'* *'Why is smoking allowed in restaurants?'* Finally: *'I was surprised that dogs are allowed into restaurants here. I have two dogs myself, but in Japan that's not allowed, they find it unhygienic. But I have to say that dogs here are well trained. They don't bite, they don't bark and they don't make a mess.'* (Japan)

'Going Dutch.'   Judging from foreigners' questions, I have the impression this custom is diminishing. But for those not familiar with these English expressions 'going Dutch' and 'a Dutch treat' both mean splitting the bill in a restaurant, each party paying his own share. The sour undertone originates from long-forgotten Anglo-Dutch hostility in the 1600s, but this quotation from the same German observer mentioned above is more recent: *'You go for dinner somewhere and afterwards all expenses must be calculated: 'He drank one beer more...' Terrible!'*

Is it really that bad? The Dutch don't agree. They 'go Dutch' because they feel equal, difference in position or income doesn't play a role, and if no special event is being celebrated no courtesies whatsoever are necessary. Such a non-occasion is apparently what the German observer witnessed (and by the way, people making a fuss about one extra beer – and they do exist – are also disliked by the Dutch!)

Glamour and elegance   In the first edition I offered this quote from an American: *'I like the smallness of things in Holland. Everything is small here, even the sky-scrapers.'* Well, things are changing; there is a desire for bigger things now. Keeping up with the international Jone-ses, creating bigger companies, demanding bigger salaries, bigger cars and even bigger buildings. In the footsteps of Rotterdam, Amster-dam and The Hague are now constructing mini-Manhattans.

In smaller businesses outside the large cities, low profile and simplicity are still appreciated. But in the internationally oriented big business that many of the readers may encounter, things are now changing very rapidly indeed. Traditional sobriety has been shaken off in this age of wealth and globalisation. And there is a definite tendency towards luxury: handmade suits, expensive cars, antiques or designer furniture, fancy office buildings with striking architecture, etc. Elsewhere you will find what might be described as 'elegant low profile'. Things may look, and be, expensive these days, but it is considered good taste to spend the money on technical quality and careful design rather than on ostentatious details. The remnants of Calvinism?

Also breaking with their national tradition some Dutch designers and architects are producing truly non-conformist and extravagant creations. Striking buildings are springing up among otherwise boring suburbs; there is a market for ultra-modern furniture and household articles. Several avant-garde young Dutch fashion designers are enjoying great success, even in Paris, but the clothes they design are mostly worn at flashy jet-set parties. If you're not invited, go and look at the photos outside the iT-disco near Amsterdam's Rembrandtplein – you will be stunned!

The more middle-of-the-road Dutch public have mixed feelings about other nations' glamour and elegance. On the one hand, their low-profile pragmatism leads them to disapprove of, even mock, other nations' lavish architecture and stylish fashion, ostentatious street life and emotional nature. But it doesn't take a psychologist to see that at the same time they envy such 'joie de vivre'. This is why so many of them eagerly travel to such fun-places, happily joining in with the local way of life.[3] Even in Holland itself recent hot summers brought out this other side of the Dutch character. An American friend of mine, back in Holland for the first time in several years, noticed the many convertible cars that have suddenly appeared on the roads. *'In this climate!?'*, she asked doubtfully… Yes, people driving convertibles like to believe that this is a Mediterranean country. Similar doubts can be expressed about the growing number of sturdy Jeeps and Landrovers in a land with about ten miles of dirt road which, for environmental reasons, are closed to motorised traffic anyway.

But back home, when autumn comes, close the roof! Whose idea was it to buy a convertible anyway? A Dutch scientist raised the following thesis: 'European unification might take a long time as long as Italian raincoats are elegant and Dutch ones waterproof.' A lady who returned to Holland after living abroad for years adds: *'It's hard to stay elegant when it's raining and there's force seven gale!'*

Expenditure for pleasure may come more easily to the Dutch nowadays, but even so, people who are perceived as underprivileged 'victims of circumstances' can still count on help from the Dutch public. Animals, landscapes and inanimate objects can also be in a position that calls for assistance. The Dutch support sports projects for the disabled, campaigns against child labour in far away countries, the survival of environmentally vulnerable nature in their own country and at the South Pole, the repair of dilapidated museums in countries even Dutch people rarely visit, and so on. Such support is given both through private donations and by government financing, and it deeply satisfies the Dutch: how useful!

Of course there are critics who point out that assistance is given on condition that at least part of the money is to be spent in Holland, or that the rain forest he has just saved may be the travel-loving Dutchman's next holiday destination. But such views somehow receive far less publicity.

Backgrounds, and counter currents   Dutch expats living in the tropics tend to analyse the laid-back pace of life there, with references to the ever-warm climate. True or not, environmental conditions in the Netherlands, the constant struggle against the waters, demand hard work and planning ahead. This was particularly so in the past, but it is still so today. Having won this battle (so far...), as a whole the Dutch are a self-confident people, with an optimistic feeling they have their fate in their own hands, and can exercise a positive influence on it if they only try hard enough. This is certainly the case now, but in fact it has always been that way. Generally speaking, they don't harbour gloomy feelings about life – think of the Portuguese *saudade*, the Hungarian *melankolia*, the Russian *nostalgiya* or *khandra,* or even the black-American *blues*. Perhaps this increase in self-confidence engendered by modern success also explains the waning in the importance of, and interest in, religion in recent decades.

After its birth in late medieval northern Italy Renaissance thinking – with its appreciation of rationality, individual achievement and practical experimentation – soon reached the trading cities of Flanders, and it also had some influence further north. During the civil war against the Spanish, Flemish Protestants – many of them merchants-fled north, bringing the Renaissance way of thinking with them and so greatly enhancing northern entrepreneurship.

The 17th century wealth of the Dutch republic stimulated scientific experimentation, and the many Dutch inventors of those days included the engineer Simon Stevin and the mathematician Huygens. The Republic also produced famous maritime explorers and cartographers. Rationalism took hold in the Netherlands. The French philosopher Descartes came here, seeking the political freedom to write on this theme, producing works which would not have been tolerated in his own country. Together with the rationalist philosopher Spinoza and the lawyer Grotius, these (and many more) people, analysing and overcoming the problems of everyday life, contributed to the economic and political needs of the Dutch republic.

Throughout the centuries the high average level of education of the people of the Netherlands has stimulated an unemotional, pragmatic approach to life, and the conviction that such a life leads to social and individual well-being. This is still true today, of course,

All in all, by tradition the Dutch mind-set is for rationality and clarity. The tendency to categorise and define the countless phenomena in life is a general human need, but the Dutch seem to have taken it quite a bit further than many other cultures. Expressions of this can be seen everywhere – in architecture, dress, working methods, the landscape. The Dutch are not very good at dealing with ambiguity and ambivalence. They like clear definitions, straight lines, sharp divisions between this and that. The Dutch have a verb – *hokjesdenken* – 'thinking in boxes'. It has a tang of disapproval to it, a suggestion of petty-bourgeois attitudes, but the phenomenon itself is widespread and widely felt to be satisfactory and productive. In spite of the paradoxes people from other countries note in Dutch behaviour and Dutch society, the Dutch perceive themselves as 'logical', 'clear', 'unambiguous'.

But even here it appears that change is underway, it seems. Although it is still by far a minority attitude, irrationality and non-'box thinking' seem to be on the increase, even in management, where training bureaux offer seminars and programmes on how to bring about and handle 'irrational processes', which supposedly bring about more creativity, innovation and profit.

This 'counter-movement' has something of a history of its own. Ever since around 1900 intellectuals and artists in the Netherlands have rebelled against too much rationality and 'squareness'; several painters and authors moved from (super-)realism to surrealism, while architects started breaking away from straight lines and box-like buildings. Significantly, a famous Dutch short story, published in 1931, describes a drab society where a dictator orders that everything be square. In the end the people rebel and return to roundness.[4]

Later, with some fleeting success, the 'youth revolt' of the 1960s and 70s tried to break open the clearly-defined 'boxes' in Dutch society and the Dutch way of thinking (like the youth in the US, using the word 'square' to indicate everything they opposed!).

Social pluriformity and nonconformism increased with mass prosperity, resulting in more and more 'box-crossing'. Many people want to, and do, break free from old conventions and restrictions, be they social, political or economic. This may confuse and irritate more conventional and older people, but the trend will probably increase now that, just like everywhere else, the non-linear virtual world of Internet and the CD-ROM is casting its spell on the Dutch economy, on education and training, and on everyday life.

1. Some time later, of course, people complained that it wasn't all that well organised. But they were Dutch.
2. *Buitenbeeld van Nederland*, Platform Beeldvorming Nederland.
3. Sometimes they take 'having fun' too far. In the summer of 2000, a number of young Dutch tourists were arrested in both Spain and Greece for harassing the general public, fighting in the street and showing disrespect for the local police.
4. *Blokken* (Blocks) by F. Bordewijk.

Chapter 7

PROCEDURES AND PLANNING

'Governing implies foreseeing'
(Dutch saying)

A finely tuned machine Most non-Dutch people see Holland as an orderly country. Indeed, with its long, straight ditches and canals, rectangular fields and neatly laid-out suburbs, the landscape does look organised. Thanks to the soft subsoil even the electricity cables, which in many countries are carried across the countryside on ugly pylons, are tidily buried underground. Roads have orderly shoulders, traffic signs indicate not only towns but also children's playgrounds, built-up areas have clearly defined limits and do not gradually fade into the surrounding countryside.

Society, too, gives an impression of being highly organised: the trains generally run on time, you can practically set your clock by the weekly refuse collection, and essential services such as water, gas and electricity rarely fail. Whether one appreciates this or not depends on personal taste, and probably also on one's experience in one's home country. Two comments: *'There is a certain order in Holland that makes things easier. Society functions well and is also quite stable. If the government changes, nothing else really changes. This order leaves you free to develop yourself the way you want to.'* (Chile) And from another side of the same continent: *'Even inside the house everything goes on schedule: dinner at six, coffee at seven. In Suriname we eat when we're hungry and we drink when we're thirsty.'* (Suriname)

As a whole, the Netherlands can be seen as a finely tuned 'machine', where rules and regulations, permits and prohibitions, time schemes and spatial planning, all contribute to keeping the economy running smoothly and to promoting the well-being of the 16 million people who live here. But such intricate machinery is delicate and vulnerable: if one thing goes wrong, a chain reaction of other events follows. A single road accident can cause traffic jams for miles around, a delayed train might upset the rail network over a wide area, a bulldozer digging in the soft soil can damage electricity cables and bring an entire town to a standstill.

Bureaucracy in a lenient society   Foreigners sometimes tell me they see Dutch society as an amazing mix of personal freedom and official bureaucracy. The freedom issue will be discussed in the next chapter, but first I want to look at the bureaucracy in Dutch life.

One complaint expatriates frequently make concerns the *red-tape* they have to face when applying for residence permits for family members, for work permits, when exchanging their national driving licence for a Dutch one, when asking for electricity, gas, cable TV, etc. to be connected. But once they settle in it may not be so bad after all, as an Australian pointed out: *'There is a lot of bureaucracy, but it seems to work here.'*

Indeed, the Town Hall, the aliens police[1], service companies, even banks and house-agents, they all require paperwork and it is frequently necessary to make several personal visits to their offices during their often limited working hours. People tell me of 'Catch-22' situations where getting one paper is not possible without the other and vice versa. Birth and marriage certificates must be sent from the home country, and translated by an authorised translator if they happen to be in a language or alphabet unknown to the Dutch. Assistance from the company's personnel department helps, but cannot prevent all the inconvenience. And in most places a foreign manager pressed for time does not take precedence over an asylum seeker who is not even allowed to work. Egalitarianism: draw a number, wait your turn, come back next Friday please.

On top of that, quite a few people who are unused to the system become irritated by functionaries, bank employees or shopkeepers answering *'Dat kan niet'* (that's impossible) if they request some transaction apparently out of the ordinary. *'Any question I seem to ask is responded to with the words, 'No, that's impossible'* (USA). Quite a few people perceive this as hostile. Now this may be cold comfort, but usually it isn't blunt unwillingness. The Dutch being 'Newtonian' and taking things literally, will respond to *exactly* what you asked, that particular option. Not very customer-oriented to begin with, and perhaps unaware of your unfamiliarity with Dutch ways, they will let *you* come up with an alternative, to which they will again reply yes or no, possible or impossible.

Another Dutch word puts foreigners off even more: *verboden!* When speaking English, most Dutchmen will translate this word as 'forbidden', because the two words seem almost identical. In fact, what they actually mean is the less harsh 'prohibited'. This linguistic error may easily irritate English native speakers, reinforcing their concept of the Dutch as blunt. I can only suggest you try your luck with bureaucracy elsewhere in the world, and then come back here and try again.

Red tape in a foreign country is always harder to handle than it is in one's own country, and certainly for first-time expatriates this can be exhausting. They wonder what is the reason behind this Dutch drive towards registration and control. Before going into that, we will explore the implications of the issue a little further.

Expatriates may not realise they are not the only ones who run up against Dutch bureaucracy. Even the bureaucratic Dutch were shocked when it recently became known that details of the average Dutch family are registered in over 900 places, or rather in 900 computers. Some of this is voluntary of course – car service stations, supermarkets, banks, insurance and health organisations, service suppliers and Internet providers, for example. But the Town Hall, a wide range of government institutions, tax and social benefit authorities, your employer and many other institutions also keep track of you. Small wonder that a law on privacy, explicitly forbidding all these computer files being linked, was passed by the Dutch parliament some years ago. Judging from a number of hilarious cases of insurmountable bureaucracy, where linked computers might well have come in handy, so far the law seems to be working. Later on we will come to see how the Dutch can accept such apparent shackles on their precious freedom.

Economic control   In all fields of the Dutch economy, too, rules, regulations and norms abound and there are controls in place. Weights and measures, licences and qualifications, percentages and time standards, quantity and quality, they are all established, put down on paper and controlled by officials who are rarely corruptible and administer the letter of the law strictly. Besides the usual ISO-norms and the like, there are strict regulations on the ecological, legal and taxation aspects of work. Needless to say, labour conditions are highly regulated too: safety and hygiene, time limits on working with computers or driving trucks, quality standards and ergonomic aspects of machines and furniture. A researcher discovered, for instance, that Dutch office workers have more direct daylight on their desks than many of their colleagues elsewhere. Since the environment, workers' rights and levels of remuneration are all important issues in the

Netherlands, people are quick to complain if they think something is wrong, and take swift action through the company council or the company doctor.

These strict controls mean that there are a great many regulations and requirements which must be complied with and this, in turn, means that setting up a business in the Netherlands is not easy either for foreign companies nor for the Dutch themselves. In recent years the process has been simplified, since self-employment has been stimulated, and there are several agencies that assist new entre-preneurs with all the red tape. Yet it is still a complicated procedure and many new small businesses fail – and not only because they misread the market. Given the importance of the correct diplomas and the proper knowledge, it is not easy for people to move from one line of business to a completely different one. Since people are supposed to be expert in their field, bankruptcy is considered shaming, and this makes it difficult to regain the trust of investors. Luckily, bankruptcies are fairly rare in these days of economic boom.

There are few fields where there are no legally laid-down regula-tions. Even hitherto totally 'free' professions such as house brokerage are now coming under official supervision, requiring licences and being subject to quality controls.

Rules on building In many residential areas it can clearly be noticed that there are limitations to the degree of fantasy architects and house-owners can apply to buildings. Obviously there are a large number of technical qualifications to construc-tion, but that's not the whole story. You may own a place, but strange colours or designs totally out of keeping with the rest of the area are neither allowed nor appreciated. Architects have to present their designs to a municipal 'aesthetics board' consisting of colleagues, local politicians and interested laymen. If their designs are too fanciful (or to dull) architects may be told to go back to the drawing board. Likewise, house owners are obliged to obtain permission to add a balcony or a roof-top extension, even a garden shed, and if they don't, the authorities are very likely to tell them to remove it, even if they have spent thousands of guilders on it. Comparing this to the haphazard architecture in his own country, with some appreciation an Egyptian called this Dutch policy: *'regulated privacy'*. On the Dutch-Belgian border you can tell from the houses which country you are in!

Only in brand-new fields such as the latest ITC and in the artistic, creative corners of society, can the limits of totally free enterprise be fully explored. Non-Dutch people are usually flabbergasted to learn that even the establishments in the Red Light District are regularly checked under the health and safety regulations and are obliged to pay their taxes, as are the 'coffee shops' which sell cannabis (these are discussed in the next chapter).

Control freaks   Coming back to more familiar terrain, when dealing with the Dutch, in business and after working hours, you will soon find that most of them are precise people. They deal with things with great attention and a keen eye for detail, applying regulations and procedures consciously (on paper) or unconsciously (with time, daily activities etc.). They themselves use terms like *Pietje Precies* ('Peter Precise') for individuals who overdo it, while some foreigners call the Dutch 'control freaks'. Others appreciate it: *'Everything here is based on time. Two o'clock is two o'clock, not earlier, not later. I like it, it's easier. You know how things will go and you can plan your day better.'* (Zambia)

Many non-Dutch nationals observe that apparently there are fixed procedures for just about everything, that there seems to be little room for improvisation, for simply taking life as it comes. Like me, not everybody likes this: *'I feel Holland to be cramped, claustrophobic. Everything is cultivated, over-organised. You can't lose your way, even in a forest here you keep seeing signs like: "To pancake restaurant turn right."* (South Africa).

At work, too, the Dutch are highly structured. Time arrangements and planning are important, verbal and written agreements should be followed up, written rules applied, details not overlooked, while in negotiations the Dutch have a reputation of arriving well-informed (and expecting their counterparts to do the same!). Some comments from widely different cultures: *'If something is not written down on paper, it doesn't exist in Holland.'* (Spanish director of an art organisation).

'In my country (Cambodia) most things are verbally agreed, in talks. Here everything is put on paper and planned long beforehand. Then you start working. And if you don't meet the planning, you have failed. In other countries they think: tomorrow is another day. The culture around meetings here is quite strange to me. They hold meetings on every subject and everything is discussed ten times over.' (Cambodia).

A Russian businessman working with Dutch people in Moscow adds: *'Compared to the Dutch, Russians seem to me rather less organised* and 'purpose oriented'. (…) It is more likely that a Russian would behave in unexpected ways (positively or negatively) than a Dutchman.'

More flexibility   Some years ago an American complained: 'Many organisations here are rigid. They are old and structured and it is very hard to change anything in their procedures. It is very difficult to convince people to change.'

Without pretending that *all* organisations have now improved on this point, it should be said that things have generally changed for the better, especially in the business world. In the face of increasing competition on the European and global scene many companies have restructured – become flatter and more flexible is the message. (In government, 'deregulation' is also taking place, although some say it could still go a lot further….)

Moreover, a more market-oriented and flexible younger generation is gradually entering the world of business. A few years ago, a Moroccan manager observed: 'Youngsters no longer expect to be cared for from the cradle to the grave. They realise they'll have to work for their money. You should see how temp-office workers do their utmost to get a permanent job. That makes me very optimistic about Holland's future.' He was right, the country is now prospering and nowadays many youngsters are no longer worried about finding a permanent job. They may enthusiastically carry on job-hopping, either through a temp-agency or independently, earning more money and doing more rewarding work with every new job.

So things have changed, but still people from American-style countries with even greater flexibility may perceive Dutch companies and the labour market as somewhat rigid. A recent remark by an American on my course: 'They must follow the structure. There is no creativity, they don't ask for anything.' A Turkish businessman also perceives a lack of creativity, adding: 'There seems to be only one way here – the way they first learned.'

Needless to say the Dutch won't be in agreement with this, but these people have a point. When the Dutch have a problem, their natural reaction is to change the procedures, not the personnel (remember they are hard to dismiss). So the result is that after a long process in which the pros and cons of every proposal are carefully debated, those same people will be applying new procedures instead of the old ones. These new procedures are intended to make things better, and one can only hope that, in reality, they are indeed more efficient than the old ones…. This may seem quite contradictory to the pragmatism described in the previous chapter, but the Dutch see it differently. They feel that by thoughtfully creating the structure of an activity, taking into account all possible unexpected circumstances, they can create an optimal setting for its actual functioning. Some people from other countries may be hard to convince that all this working on procedures is efficient: *'They lose a lot of time with bad organisation.'* (Germany) But others observe that the success of the Dutch economy is not so much a matter of the Dutch working harder than other nationalities, but the effect of them organising their work more efficiently.

Meetings   Do you recall the American's remark: *'Let's stop talking about it and DO something?'* I wasn't around of course, but I'm sure the Dutch looked up from their debate with some amazement: what is Johnson talking about? They *were* doing something, something very useful! They felt that thoughtfully talking over the problem would ensure potential mishaps would be avoided – so they were being very productive. To the Dutch, 'talking' is not a totally different thing than 'doing'; it is an important and integral part of it!

Meetings, of which there are many, are highly structured, with fixed agendas. Someone is appointed to the chair and sometimes an extra 'time-watcher' is designated. The minutes of the previous meeting are briefly discussed before new points are raided. Minutes of this meeting are taken, later they will be distributed and discussed at the next meeting.

Besides meetings themselves following fixed procedures, they tend to produce more procedures, in order to satisfy the various views given by the participants. As I mentioned when discussing the issue of directness, given that participants come well prepared and are expected to state their views strongly, it may take quite some time before compromise is reached. Dutch meetings can last a long time. *'I wouldn't mind missing the Dutch meeting culture. If you phone someone, unavoidably the answer is: he's in a meeting, can you phone again? That disturbed me right from the beginning of my stay. They only meet here for the sake of meeting. The positive side is that everyone is seeking consensus with one another, although often the opinions are fixed beforehand. It becomes a charade, a ritual, sponsored by coffee producers.'* (Germany)

Generally speaking, the Dutch feel that all this leads to good products, solid quality standards and satisfied workers who feel involved, but outsiders may be shocked: *'There are so many procedures, to me they are a stumbling block. There is not much give and take here.'* (Singapore) There *is* give and take, but it all happens during those meetings. The real negotiating takes place *in* meetings, not before, in the corridors, although of course alliances may be sought there. *'In meetings, there is endless talking from everyone, with no clear ends or actions.'* (France)

It is true that the procedures of Dutch meetings can be confusing (and not only to the non-Dutch), topics appearing on the agenda time and time again and any real decisions postponed. Nonetheless, the participants *do* have clear ends in mind. Although it may indeed take a long time to reach, the eventual decision will be optimally satisfying to all the parties involved. A lot depends on the discipline of the participants and the qualities of the appointed chairperson. If (s)he is not strict enough, topics may take far longer to discuss than expected and others have to wait until the next meeting. Given the outspoken opinions, it may take quite some time and several meetings before everyone is convinced that this or that compromise is the most acceptable. The Dutch use the word 'massage' for this slow process. Even when a decision is finally made, people coming up with powerful arguments can reopen the whole discussion: *'We reached consensus at the meeting, but the next day an e-mail was sent saying that they disagreed.'* (US businessman).

Time and *agendas*   *'The Dutch are perfectionists, they are too strict in their demands. I also find them rigid in their dealing with time. To them it becomes an end rather than a means.'* (A Pakistani exporter to Holland)

Yes, the Dutch are strict about time. Now that everybody has a mobile phone there is no excuse for not calling if you are likely to be delayed. If you are five minutes late for a personal meeting, nothing will be said, and ten minutes is excusable. But more than that calls for abject and extensive apologies: the traditional excuse was 'the bridge was open', nowadays it is traffic jams and delayed trains. By the way, arriving early is not much appreciated either and the Dutch will just make you wait. Why this obsession with time, some might ask, what's the point?

The point is that Dutch culture is a typical example of a 'monochronic' culture, meaning: one thing at a time. It is sometimes surprising to people from some other cultures to find that the usual time allocated to a first meeting is one full hour. Every minute you are late means one minute less of the time your counterpart allocated to you. When the hour is over, it is over. Other people, who have come to discuss other subjects, will be waiting to see your counterpart. 'Monochronic' people are not very good at combining two things in one, unlike 'polychronic' people such as Italians and people from other southern cultures. Two different things or two different people at one time make the Dutch uneasy and irritable, in their private life, too. The good thing is that you get your counterpart's full attention. During your meeting other people will be kept away and even telephone calls may be put on hold. So, among themselves the Dutch will say things like 'Ah, good, you're right on time!'. It deeply satisfies the Dutch to be on time or to have things ready at the time appointed or planned. Calendars and clocks play a major role in Dutch society, as do their daily agendas.

Virtually all the Dutch, starting when they are still schoolchildren, carry an *agenda*, their diary (or organiser) full of pre-printed dates and hours. Nothing in Dutch life, whether at work or at home, happens without consulting the agenda. You want to see me now to discuss proposal? In half an hour I can spare five minutes. Ah, you need longer than that? Wait, I'll just check my agenda.

It wasn't so bad some twenty years ago, but since then, everybody's life has grown into a carefully managed time project. *Druk-druk-druk*, remember? Just about all companies and organisations provide courses on time management. One common measure is a precise notation of the time a meeting starts and finishes. This system has extended from expensive paid-by-the-hour professionals such as lawyers and consultants, to other activities and levels in the company. This consciousness of time increases people's feeling of being pressured. Many people feel so *druk* that the Ministry of Health has coined a rather ugly term promoting a change in life-style: *onthaasten*, 'de-hurrying'. But unless there is suddenly a major change in their career prospects, few people feel able to follow this advice – except for those who didn't need it in the first place. In a later chapter we will see what all these people do with their lives after work.

Time schedules are also strictly adhered to in general daily life. Coming back to the issue of customer service: shops and public facilities have signs indicating the opening hours, and one should count on such establishment following these punctually. Don't think for a moment that you will get in five minutes sooner, even when the shopkeeper or the official is clearly there already. *'In my country, when you smile through the window, they will open up for you again!'* (Ukraine). In Holland your smile needs to be exceptionally warm because shops opening early risk a fine! And if you walk into a shop two minutes before closing time don't expect the assistants to fall over themselves to serve you! The shops know the rules, the workers know their rights, and private life is sacrosanct (see chapter 8). If you're late, it's your problem!

Overtime   *'The Dutch don't like to work very hard, they never work longer than required.'* (Japan). Hmm, this is the second quote referring to perceived laziness among the *druk-druk-druks*. Well, everything is relative. Especially at lower levels, people may not work one minute longer than required, things should be done by 5PM. But during the hours they do work they work quite hard and only take short breaks.

Again, workers are very well aware of their rights and duties. High work ethics and responsibility make them work hard (yes, including those meetings…), but a high appreciation for leisure time plus strong family-orientation make most of them stick to the official working hours. The phenomenon of staying at the workplace just to please the boss or impress one's colleagues – current in other countries – is not widespread in Dutch firms.

Overtime is not popular, even paid overtime. Senior managers, of course, work overtime, sometimes working 70, 80 hours a week or more. They take their work home, and carry notebooks and laptops so as not to lose a single valuable minute. But requiring administrative or blue-collar workers to work overtime should be kept to a minimum. With the present labour shortage overtime is increasing, but the CAO will probably order that it be paid, or compensated for by additional days off. In organisations forced to make strict economies payment for overtime might be out of the question and workers may have as many as 100 days of compensation due, but no time to enjoy them! Some commercial firms have now introduced a policy of 'buying back' these holidays, in order not to lose desperately needed workers.

Stress, burn-out and the WAO   In spite of the Japanese view expressed above, the Dutch do suffer from stress, and a great deal of it, both at management levels, among ordinary employees and private entrepreneurs. An estimated 10% of the workforce suffer from stress and burnout (the Dutch also use these English words), and so they are considered a very serious issue both in organisations and in the health care sector. Consultancy agencies organise management workshops on them, and even TV programmes try to assist companies, organisations and individuals in preventing it. Almost-empty monasteries and trendy health resorts offer people opportunities for 'getting away from it all'.

Stress and burnout are among the main reasons for going into the 'WAO' (the Labour Disability Benefit, pronounced way-ah-oh). This benefit, which is paid out after people have been officially sick for one year, entitles them to 70% of their last salary. The WAO benefit is not all that unique and is paid in other western Europe countries. But the percentage of the Dutch workforce that receive it is the highest in Europe. For years it has been paid out to numbers of workers ranging between 600.000 and (let's err on the cautious side) 990.000. In a labour market of some 7 to 8 million people, the present number is again approaching one million – more than 13% of the workforce. Only Sweden and France come anywhere near this figure. Fortunately, not all of them are 'in de WAO' a full hundred percent, but even so, it can be seen as the dark side of the Dutch model, highly controversial and problematic.

Set up in the 1970s for strictly work-related illness or injury, over the years WAO has developed into a major trap for any worker who is medically diagnosed as being 'unfit' for work, whether physically or psychologically. Broken legs, chronic ache in the lower back, RSI (mouse arm), ME (chronic fatigue), they all count. Now before you start thinking: 'the Japanese was right, they *are a* lazy lot', remember that in a society where work is highly valued, most circles consider being 'in the WAO' to be shaming. Many people in this position become the object of other people's disapproval, and it often leads to them suffering from low-self esteem, a sense of uselessness or depression. Thus, being in the WAO may make matters even worse and lead to people joining the hard-core 'long-term unemployed', a fairly constant number of some 200.000 people.

Some employers tend to speculate on the low work ethic of some people in the WAO. Of course the system is abused, with quite healthy people, some even working 'black', receiving benefit. But reversing the charge, trade unions point out that it also offers employers an easy way of getting rid of difficult-to-discharge and expensive personnel. The WAO makes it possible to get rid of 'difficult' or surplus workers on medical grounds, costing employers little money, since the benefit is mostly funded by the workers and the state. Whatever the truth of the matter, every time the number approaches the million mark, alarm bells ring in The Hague, as happened again in 2000, when it was said that such sick leave always indicates deeper problems in a company. After such a fresh analysis, revised plans, projects and policies are launched in an attempt to reduce it. Employers are sanctioned for letting workers slip into the WAO, or offered subsidies to take on people receiving WAO benefit. Part of the cost of this benefit is now being charged to employers. It has also been proposed that WAO benefit should only be paid after an employee has been unfit for work for *three* years.

The strange situation that has now come about is that some of the Dutch work too hard and would like to work less, while others don't work at all and would like to. With the present situation of almost full employment, obviously this 'hidden unemployment' is seen as a reservoir that should be tapped, but this will not be easy. One reason is that the shortage of doctors makes re-examination and re-assessment a long process, while not everyone in the WAO is qualified for the high demands of the present-day labour market. And, of course, a number of them are really very ill, or by now lack the flexibility or up-to-date knowledge needed to rejoin the labour market. A fairly large element are older workers from the ethnic groups, while younger women also run a higher risk of getting into WAO. All in all, it is a stressful situation for employers, workers and politicians alike.

Planning Coming back to the time-issue – a final aspect of this is planning. The Dutch try to keep everything under control, even the future. In a stable, well-organised society this may not be as difficult as it is in some others, but it still takes careful planning to achieve it. So the Dutch do just that. *'In Holland they prefer to deal with risk as a calculated risk.'* (Russia) The Dutch indeed have several old expressions cautioning care: 'Don't skate over one night's ice', and 'Be careful, so the line won't break'. Additional proof is provided by the fact that all companies and virtually all individuals[2] in the Netherlands have insurance for just about anything that might go amiss in life.

In business, the Dutch plan is to allocate a realistic amount of time and money for every part of the procedure, and as they go along check whether it fits in with the reality of the situation. If it doesn't – which usually causes them a good deal of concern – the message is change the plan and reschedule. Evaluation is an important element of this process because one can learn from it, especially when the outcome is critical and 'constructive' – and direct. (Friendly feedback like 'excellent', which is considered polite in some countries, may make you feel good, but doesn't stimulate improvement!) Critical evaluation is carried out all the time, everywhere, and taken very seriously.

Obviously, those 100 hours of compensating overtime indicate that it doesn't always work, but still: planning, establishing the exact criteria, monitoring, evaluating and planning again, that is the way. The Dutch term for this is *beleid*, an often-used word in companies and organisations alike. It translates as 'policy', but it encompasses not only the aim to reach targets, but also the underlying vision and the practical procedures put in place to reach them. One of the worst criticisms in a company – horizontally or bottom-up – is that management has a wrong *beleid* – or worse, none at all – implying that either there is no realistic and/or inspiring vision for the future or, if there is, management didn't think through all the practical implications.

Nowadays companies and organisations are encouraged to structure *beleid* (and details of it) in a 'pro-active' way: think in advance of every potential development or mishap that might influence the outcome, so that you can immediately react and adjust the plan to the new reality. The Dutch don't even feel it to be a particularly unusual procedure; it comes naturally to them. They may even apply the principle in their private lives. All in all, with plenty of money to spend and little time to enjoy it, time is money no longer; time is much *more* than money.

Of course things do go wrong sometimes. Given all the rules and regulations, people will immediately ask: how come? In the past, people simply accepted individuals' and organisations' apologies for mistakes. Nowadays, perhaps under American influence, they may start legal proceedings seeking compensation or damages, particularly if the other party is perceived as rich. But for the readers' peace of mind it should be said that, so far, judges here tend to grant far lower amounts of compensation or damages than their US colleagues do. Most Dutch people still smile when they see all the overly cautious directions for use on some foreign products, and if someone trips over a loose carpet at a friend's house and breaks his leg he rarely considers suing that friend for damages. But the trend is there…

Some context   The Netherlands could be seen as a finely tuned machine balancing countless social, economic, natural and legal aspects. Although the Dutch do appreciate (some) challenge and adventure, as will be discussed in the next chapter, they don't want it at home. There they prefer safety and cosiness[3], full control of their own lives, security. Living in a small country, lacking vast forests or wild mountains, there are no places where people can *not* maintain control: *'I don't like the flat scenery here, there are no surprises. You feel like God: you can control everything and see everyone's activities.'* (Ireland)

Of course the Dutch do have their natural environment under control, with very few exceptions (floods, climate). Keeping an area below sea level dry and arable implies quite a lot of organising – of people, of materials, of funds. Modern water control in the Netherlands involves a mighty ministerial organisation (with regional and local departments) allocated an annual budget of billions of Euros, and highly professional engineers graduating from specialised universities.

Perhaps this explains how the Dutch became organised initially. As early as the 17th century precise lists and schedules were used in commercial activities, and present day bureaucracy may be merely an extension of this. Be that as it may, the Dutch do believe in control, in security. Not only government and business circles apply these methods, even private people (consciously or not) do it, in their finances, their career, their housing, their household. Dutch banks supply the general public with booklets on how to invest in shares, how to best provide for old age, how to finance their children's education, and so on.

Controlled 'irregularity'   Even 'chaos' is controlled in Holland: for environmental reasons formerly cultivated land is being given back to nature, bulldozed back into wilderness. In some places old river dikes have been broken open to allow the river to return to its natural meandering course and to create safe spillover areas - both of which lessen the risk of floods. Water engineers, biologists and others are involved in the careful planning and monitoring of such processes. It is estimated that between 2000 and 2050, on top of the normal budget for water control, the country will need an extra 11 billion euros and 60.000 hectares of land to make Dutch inland waters less harmful and more natural.

Bored by the rectangularity of suburban building and infra-structure, municipal architects are now designing 'spontaneously' meandering roads, and houses with turrets and other irregular

shapes. In parks and other natural areas, small hills are sometimes created to break the flat monotony. An example on a
smaller scale: Amsterdam is encouraging nature to return to
some of the city's waterways by creating 'natural' rafts where
birds, rare insects and plants may find a habitat.

To people from other cultures all this order may sound terribly boring
and calculating (and some locals agree), but it deeply satisfies most
Dutch people who see it as a clear path to the future. And if you don't
agree with them, they will point out to you how successful they have
been by applying such procedures. They have the facts to prove it.
There is good and fairly cheap education for everyone, long, paid
holidays for most people, a very high rate of car ownership and yet
good public transport, the world's lowest percentage of teenage
pregnancies, etc. But at what cost, you might well ask. Well, yes, at
the cost of detailed registration, specific procedures for almost everything, permits and licences needed for a host of things, an official
stamp here, an official signature there, and all the rest of the dreary
bureaucratic hassle. And of course: high taxation! Not everyone likes
it: *'The state is too strong here, it invades your life with so many rules. But
everybody seems to happily obey and pay their taxes. I find this strange.'*
(From Luxembourg, to my surprise)

*'The state is something big and heavy that lies on top of you, here. A
friend of mine is pregnant and these healthcare people came round to inspect
the house. She didn't like that, and I told her: just tell them NO.* (Argentinean lady, not realising that in Holland delivering the baby with the
assistance of a professional midwife in the friendly comfort of one's
own home is the preferred norm. But the health authorities do indeed
want to check whether both the mother's health and the general
household situation allow for it.)

If given the chance the Dutch set up private organisations in ways
quite similar to those of the state: be it street committees, church
organisations, charitable bodies or hobby clubs, they all have rules, a
president, a treasurer, a secretary to take the minutes, a time plan
with targets, etc. At the same time their meetings are a social
occasion with good conversation and plenty of coffee.

Freedom secured: out of control   Again we come to a paradox,
for even Dutch rules have their exceptions! In this well (over?-) organised country, you will see cyclists ignoring traffic lights all the time

(I have to admit I'm one of them), while car drivers overtake you on the right (thus, the wrong!) side at a speed far above the legal limit (which I don't). You will see people throwing litter under a sign telling them not to, and dogs being allowed to relieve themselves on the pavement. Another recent cause of irritation is people in trains using their mobile phones to talk loudly about their private concerns. Generally speaking, courteous behaviour is hard to find these days. Are these those same rule-abiding Dutchmen we just talked of? What is this, a general decay of society, the breakdown of good manners, a disdain for the political decision-making process that one finds in many Western countries, or what?

'We (Russians) also have that combination of rationalism and anarchism, so typical in the Dutch. But with the Dutch, rationalism dominates and anarchism is deep down, while in Russia both anarchism and rationality are at the surface.' (Russia)

It may appear to some readers that bureaucracy, rules and regulations are the main goal in life to the Dutch, but they're not, really. They are, or should be, a practical means of achieving and maintaining the security to live the way they want. So once they feel this freedom is secured, the rules can be set aside. If this doesn't happen officially, people will just ignore them and go their own way. This happens especially in situations where nobody knows you, where your peer group is not around, but not at home, not in one's own street, not at work. It confuses foreigners: *'Some rules are broken, others are not. Why?'* (Britain)

In public, outside their own social box, the orderly Dutch can be quite anarchistic or even aggressive: in traffic, at railway stations, in supermarket check-out queues, in anonymous places which might be downtown or only be a few streets away from home. Maybe it's also just an outlet for repressed emotions and creativity. Just like everywhere else, whether people behave badly or not depends on personal style, the degree of inner civilisation, the day and age they live in, and many other factors. Many people from other countries (and with them the politer element of the Dutch population) certainly cannot appreciate it: *'Dutch people never get out of your way, they are physically close by to you. I don't like that.'* (Australia) and: *'People are pushy here, more so than in Belgium or Germany. People in shops are downright rude.'* (USA) A German who just arrived from a long stay in Italy said: *'The Dutch have a southern way of driving.'* A 2000 survey[4] confirmed that (after the British) in traffic the Dutch are the second rudest Europeans:

80% of them have experienced obscene gestures; a large percentage flash their headlights to signal others to move aside; and – what many find the most irritating of all – tailgating (driving much too close to the car in front) seems to be a national pastime.

After first apologising, may I hint at the difference in size and population density between the observers' countries and my own, and remind them that a 'comfortable physical distance' is also a culturally determined factor? May I also refer back to the paragraph on stress and work-pressure? Yes, it is true that one regularly see examples of impolite and antisocial behaviour. They are expressions of highly individualistic attitudes, a disregard for other people's comfort, and the individual culprits will probably come up with vague excuses of 'urgent appointments' and 'stress'. Needless to say, all this has led to public complaints by politicians and the man in the street about the loss of discipline and good manners. Even the Queen has mentioned it in one of her Christmas speeches. But none of it seems to help very much: *'You cannot move a centimetre here or you run into someone. And all those masses of people, so many people. I sometimes feel like a fish swimming against the current, against all those swarms of people, while I want to watch everything at my ease.'* (Iceland).

Two more quotes on Dutch spatial behaviour: *'Driving is difficult here, with narrow streets and canals, and bicycles all over you.'* (Canada). *'Everything is small here: the shops, the refrigerators, the houses, the toilets, the showers.'* (Iran)

Backgrounds   Again, there are backgrounds to these attitudes. The major one, deep down, may well be that the Netherlands is a very successful nation, so there is little incentive or stimulus for people to change their ways. And, of course, there's a history to it as well.

Remember the *waterschappen* discussed earlier? Lacking a central government to do it for them, local inhabitants were forced to set up organisations to build and maintain dykes to keep the waters of the seas and rivers at bay. Everyone's contribution of work, money and materials was recorded in detail. Small-scale solutions, in regions where everybody knew everybody else. In drier areas, feudal landlords registered peasants' contributions (and shortcomings), while in the cities taxes were levied through equally precise methods. Organisations were in private hands and were basically interested in financial registration, business administration, so to speak – still a popular study. Reports of meetings of all kinds and lists of contributions dating back to the late Middle Ages are still kept in Dutch archives and museums. The same is true of the cargoes carried by the Dutch East India Company (VOC) and the West India Company (WIC), both founded in the early 1600s. Significantly, several Asian languages took their bookkeeping terminology from the VOC, while Sri Lanka is still proud of having 'Dutch Roman Law'.

In a way, Dutch society was created by its inhabitants, without much influence from authorities high up. Apparently some people still sense this: *'The Dutch are very proud of their political culture, of their talent to get things done and to find negotiable solutions to their problems. They have a special feeling for practicality, based on self-confidence and trust in others, authority included. At the same time they know that authorities can make mistakes too. This gives them a kind of tolerance towards other people's failures, and space to act for themselves.'* (Brazil)

As for civic behaviour – remember the country was a federal republic. There was neither a royal court nor any another centralised authority setting the overall standard. The ancient nobility (where it still existed) no longer had much influence, and the rich merchants lived a life beyond other people's means and couldn't really set an example either. Cities and provinces enacted temporal laws to define and punish criminal and antisocial behaviour, but far more important than these 'earthly' laws were the norms and values of the Bible, which served as guidelines for most people. This left moral judgement largely to one's religious peer group, and to God of course. Cleanliness was next to godliness, and this was reflected in the impeccable Dutch houses and an almost hysterical mania for cleaning which foreign visitors were already commenting upon centuries ago. Even today the traditional open curtains invite you to inspect how orderly and decent the inhabitants are, a kind of voluntary social control. (You may glance in passing, but you are not supposed to stop and stare!)

During these centuries the state was almost absent from people's private lives. Up until about 1800 it was the churches which kept family registers. Then, under Napoleontic rule, the state introduced fixed family names and house numbers and delegated the task of registration to the Town Halls. Gradually, more personal registration crept in. In the 19th century, the Dutch state was dominated by liberals, who were against too much state interference, leaving welfare to the churches. But by 1890 this had changed, industrialisation meant that working conditions, city housing and education had to be regulated. First Christian-democratic and then Social-democratic influence grew, and the first social benefits were set up to fight for workers' rights and against urban poverty. Soon, housing projects were set up by organisations affiliated to trade unions, and they needed data on the size of families, income, etc. in order to ensure a just allocation.

During the Second World War, the detailed registration of citizens' private affairs, including religion, made the persecution of Dutch Jewry very easy, with the effect that the post-war generation was very sensitive to too much government influence in this area. In the early 1970s a census had to be cancelled because too many people openly refused to take part.

After the social changes which occurred in the 1970s people generally began to trust the government again. Corruption is rare in Holland, the press is omnipresent and free, the state annually accounts for all its expenditure, and anyone can see that benefits are distributed as fairly as possible. Generally speaking, the politicians do listen to citizens' complaints (if they don't, or don't react quickly enough, there are several measures which can be taken). And in order to maintain this status quo and to prevent, as far as possible, abuse by both natives and immigrants, precise registration of everyone and everything is necessary. Moreover, with increased immigration, there is public pressure on the authorities to combat abuse of the social benefit system. Don't forget that once people from other countries are finally registered here, they may also reap the benefits of this system. Strange that I never hear expatriates complain about the generous child allowances they receive in the Netherlands....

All this brings us to the next chapter, on tolerance and indifference in a pleasure society.

1. This name makes expats feel far from home, but it is older than the movie of the same title.
2. Major exceptions are people from ethnic groups and some fiercely orthodox Calvinists.
3. 'Gezellig', see chapter 6.
4. Sept. 2000, by Gallup International, interviewing 10.000 drivers in 16 European countries.

Chapter 8

THE PLEASURE SOCIETY TOLERANT OR INDIFFERENT?

'Freedom = happiness' (Dutch saying)

This chapter, critical Dutch readers might say, is not really relevant to business people who whizz from the airport to a business lunch, from a factory visit to a meeting, and then back to Schiphol. But not everyone is such a workaholic and many business people take at least some time to see a bit more of the country they visit, to get a taste of the local culture. Moreover, not all business people are business *travellers*. Readers may have been be posted to Holland, some may have lived here for several years, and they cannot fail to have noticed some aspects of the subject of this chapter – the way the Dutch enjoy life, the apparently unlimited freedom and the tolerant attitudes towards freedom.

Authority   As we saw in a previous chapter, in Dutch society people expect and demand to be able to judge matters for themselves and to make their own decisions. Generally speaking, they dislike social obligations or any other claims which infringe on their personal freedom. Financial debt is felt to do this, as do unannounced visits, social niceties and conventions about dress, and the possible demands which dealing with hierarchy might impose. They wish to be their own maters, only following authorities if these have proven to be worthy of loyalty.

One notices few policemen in the streets, and outside the barracks military uniforms can only be seen when soldiers travel home. Uniforms in general are felt to be pompous and slightly ridiculous, certainly for people without any real authority, such as waiters or clerks. (Remember: content is important in Dutch culture, not external appearance!) *'People here don't seem to feel much respect for police officers or for people in uniforms. They just talk to them or ask questions. It is all very simple and open, very normal.'* (Argentine) *'Especially Amsterdam is very liberal. But not just liberal, there is a simple logic to it. For instance: riding a bike in a one-way street against the traffic. In the beginning, when I saw someone do that, I thought: how can you do that! Now I know: it is the quickest way. When I myself did it the first time – I felt rather wicked – a police car saw me and the officer gestured towards me. So I started apologising, but he just said: look, we're coming from the right side, you from the wrong, so move over a bit. That was all! Just plain logical.'* (UK)

Dutch authorities know that they are subject to critical inspected by the public and behave accordingly: a low profile. If they can solve problems through calm discussion, they will usually do so, knowing that afterwards the people with the problem will still be around.

Crime-prevention is considered just as important and effective as crime-solving. The traffic police announce speed checks on the radio, with the aim of persuading drivers to reduce their speed rather than catching and fining the maximum number of speeding motorists.

The police only use their full powers in more extreme cases, using violence if really necessary. But that is rare, and mostly restricted to dealing with violent criminals, football hooligans and the like. (After the Amsterdam police struck out at young, non-violent demonstrators at the 1997 EU summit, the 'victims' took them to court, which decided that the demonstrators had been unlawfully attacked and gave them an indemnification!) As a matter of fact, the Netherlands doesn't have many police officers or private security guards per head of population. In 1996 there were fewer than 400 per 100,000 people, compared to over 500 in Germany, over 600 in the U.K. and Canada, and almost 1,000 in the USA. Part of this might be attributed to problems in finding suitable recruits, but in my opinion it also reflects the non-authoritarian character of Dutch society.

So, generally speaking, people live the way they want to live, especially in the larger cities. There are limits, of course, but they are broad and determined by laws based on compromise, and within them there is much freedom for highly individual behaviour, and little repression. *'I've worked in many countries, the Middle East, Asia, Australia, the USA, but I like working in Holland best. In no other country do you find so much personal freedom, both at work and outside.'* (Belgium)

Live your own life   In the cities, in particular, all kinds of life-styles are openly practised and there are wide-ranging political views, artistic tastes, sexual preferences, and so on. It is all quite visible in public behaviour, in fashion, in hairstyles, and in countless other ways. City centres are full of unusual characters, while street posters announce parties that are obviously going to be wild.

Not everyone – whether a native or from another country – appreciates every aspect of this freedom and explicitness, but it is widely felt to be a basic human right. People may smile at what they see, shrug their shoulders indifferently or criticise sourly, but interference is considered 'intolerant' and is frowned upon. Unfortunately, after a number of serious cases of random violence (see below), intervening between violent people and their victims is now considered hazardous, too. But most of the time there is an abundance of social and personal freedom: *'Here in Holland I have space to breathe.*

I can lead my own life. Nobody troubles me. I feel one among many. I love that freedom. Life here is as it should be. I like the way everybody here is independent.' (Tanzania)

There are more critical views, too. The French 'Le Monde' correspondent wrote: *'The Netherlands is not the modern country it loves to be, experimenting with social issues. But it is a country where you can feel free as a citizen on the condition that you can accept the pressure of social control, don't stand out too much and especially behave 'normal'.* And, from a different angle: *'There is so much freedom and permissiveness here that sometimes it causes clashes between us and our children.'* (India)

Fun, fun, fun Do you remember the Italian saying, *'The Dutch have other ways of enjoying themselves'*? Yes, they have. There has been an enormous growth in recent years in what we might term the 'fun sector'. All over the country organisations of all kinds set up spectacular events of a more or less commercial nature, announced through radio commercials, and eagerly supported by local shopkeepers and cafe owners. Most are meant to attract families with children, but some cater for quite special categories of visitors.

When it's not quite their cup of tea, passers-by will watch with a mixture of amused smiles, curious looks or embarrassed glances, but taking any action against people with a different lifestyle than your own is simply not done. With the exception of certain football matches such spectacles take place in a harmonious, non-violent atmosphere, observed from the sidelines by smiling police officers. Here we will mention only a few of these festivities.

The largest event organised so far was Sail 2000, the visit to Amsterdam of dozens of 'tall ships' and countless other sailing vessels. This event attracted three million people in three days and was largely incident free. Another example is the 'Fast Forward Dance Parade' in downtown Rotterdam, August 2000: it blasted 400.000 watts of sound amplification at an estimated 300.000 participants and spectators. That was only a few weeks after the annual Caribbean street festival, an imitation of Rio de Janeiro's carnival, in which thousands of both ethnic and Dutch hips swayed in tropical ecstasy. Beside the traditional royal tour in September, The Hague has the annual North Sea Jazz Festival. Its suburb of Scheveningen witnesses the festive entry of the year's first barrels of herring, and organises kite flying competitions, sandcastle building, and other seaside-related activities.

The downside is that all these events create traffic jams for miles around, put a great strain on public transport and may result in overcrowded streets, cafés and restaurants, and a great deal of noise and litter.

Amsterdam   'Ah, Dutch savages!?', a man from Rwanda humorously commented, on seeing some rather fantastically attired youngsters as I showed him round central Amsterdam. Every year millions of tourists are intrigued by the Dutch capital, with its unusual mix of old elegance and very modern lifestyles, and the freedom to enjoy both: 'I prefer Amsterdam to Venice. Venice is beautiful too, but Amsterdam is ALIVE!' (New Zealand). Amsterdam's inhabitants are proud of their city to the point of chauvinism, while people elsewhere in Holland either see it as an attractive place to do what they cannot do close to home, or as a dangerous place full of pickpockets and prostitutes.

There is so much to do these days in Amsterdam that its inhabitants have started complaining and demanding 'give us back our city!' With centuries of history as a very international port behind it, Amsterdam offers just about anyone and everyone the chance to live the way they want. People from abroad don't always appreciate it – an American woman on my programme used the term 'raunchy' – but most people are rather fascinated, especially by the widely publicised aspects of drugs and sex, which are just two aspects of the city's wide variety.

'In Amsterdam they like art (...). I appreciate Amsterdam a lot: it offers me knowledge and culture, it is a cultured city. It is easy for me to live and work here. Especially these last few years: the city is getting more inter-national and I find that people must think internationally.' (Hong Kong)

'No, coming from Tokyo to Amsterdam was not like coming to a village. Amsterdam has it, Tokyo doesn't. Tokyo is nice to look at, but in an artificial, superficial way. People there are interested only in buying things, clothes especially. Amsterdam may be more gross on the outside, not as sophistic-ated, but there is more culture, it goes deeper.' (Japan)

Some of the 'Amsterdam freedom' has spread to other cities, and even to villages. Foreigners react in amusement or shock, reflecting very much what they are or aren't used to at home. 'We see people at bus stops almost romancing each other. That looks odd to us.' (Nigerian couple living in The Hague)

'A Dutch norm that the Japanese could adopt is the tolerance and openness. (...) Seeing something new, the Dutch think: hey, maybe that's nice, maybe we can do something with that, let's take a closer look.'

Political system: pluriformity

It is difficult to understand this tolerance, this freedom, these liberal attitudes (and this disdain of other people's feelings), without looking at the broad outlines of the political system.

It was only after 1795 that a centralised political system was introduced in the Netherlands, first still as a republic, but soon as a French puppet kingdom under Napoleon's younger brother Louis. The hitherto autonomous 'states' became provinces of a more unified state. After 1813 it emerged as an independent country again, under the now royal House of Orange-Nassau. By 1848, the role of the king was restricted under the dominance of the liberals, while after the 1880s, more political and religious pluriformity took root in the Dutch political system. Several Christian and socialist parties sprang up beside the liberals, each representing a clearly defined section of the population. None ever attained an overall majority, and all governments were coalitions of two or more parties, each party keeping in mind their own interests, weighing the pros and cons of every proposal. Compromise had to be reached before any action could be taken. Firmly stating one's own position, listening critically to the views of others, and finally adding 'water to the wine', became the norm.

Nowadays, with more than 20 political parties participating in each national election, this is still the case. Some five or six of these parties play a major role at a national level, but locally others may be important, too. Most people vote for a party voicing their view, rather than for an individual politician, and politicians' private lives or income are mostly unknown to the general public. Being openly hungry for power is frowned upon: act normal, use your talents for the good of all, and don't make a fuss about it, remember? It may be interesting to know that most Dutch politicians come from government or in higher education rather than from the business world.

Pluriformity was given a fresh start with the rapid social changes that began in the 1960s. In just thirty years the country saw the break-up of the former small-scale society. The existing clearly defined groups, with a large degree of personal contact and internal control, gave way to a far more anonymous and mostly urban society where individuals followed very different and often opposing lifestyles.

This was not essentially unique, of course, it occurred in all western societies, but perhaps the effect was a little stronger in the Netherlands. One effect of pluriformity is that there is always at least one party prepared to annex any new social problem or a forgotten group of underprivileged people. They will bring the problem before parliament and come up with proposals to solve it, trying to find support from the other parties. Then the Dutch circus of compromise is set in motion and, if agreement is finally reached, in the end various amounts of money will be allocated to help solve the problem, procedures might be changed, and committees set up to oversee the whole process. It is, of course, all very democratic and people from quite a few other countries might be envious, but in the Netherlands it also leads to complaints about 'buying off problems'.

Lifestyles and intolerance   On individual levels, people can choose from a wide range of lifestyles, based on various combinations of factors to do with class and income, religious or political views, personal preferences and subcultures. People may also participate in all kinds of organisations based on some joint activity or interest: a charity, a hobby or a course of study. Finally, on a more abstract level, but still uniting people of a particular mind-set, many people have long-term subscriptions to a particular newspaper or television broadcaster, and this links subscribers in an invisible religious or ideological network.

The overall result is a patchwork society in which people half-consciously define themselves according to their affiliations, with covert 'in-group' feelings, them and us. Under Dutch circumstances, all these groups are minorities, so they are forced to put up with each other. This means that as a whole Dutch society may appear to be one of great tolerance, but on more individual levels this is not always the case.

For much of their lives people stick to their group, though it is becoming increasingly popular nowadays to move from one group to another. Each group has its norms and values, its approved standard behaviour and its frowned-upon deviations. In public, Dutch people don't always openly comment on this, but in private they will certainly make known their opinion on groups they feel to be different from theirs. This is also done in the presence of foreign nationals, often to their surprise or even dismay. It may strike them as outright intolerant, or at least inconsistent: *'They think they're liberal but they are conservative really.'* (USA) And the former ambassador of South Africa added: *'My personal experience in the Netherlands is that 'tolerance' is a rather dualistic concept. On the one hand (and that is so confusing about Dutch society) there is an incredible amount of tolerance. Yet, at the same time people are very quick to jump to strong intolerant opinions.'* Well, remember (from chapter 6) the rather unambiguous way of thinking of many Dutch people: this or that, yes or no, good or bad. On individual levels people may indeed not be at all tolerant. It is only in the process of reaching compromise that tolerance and the ambiguity and vagueness related to it arises.

An American book on European-American differences[1] states that Europeans define themselves through 'meaningful conversation'. That is certainly true of the Dutch, who, when making the acquaintance of new neighbours or colleagues like to find out who the other party is, by discussing fairly profound or personal subjects. The inquisitiveness may involve religious or political subjects, ideas on life in general and our own in particular, philosophies on society and the modern age, anything and everything is grist to the mill.

Some foreigners take this to be sheer nosiness, an unpleasant intrusion into their privacy. On top of that, they often see the Dutch as *'argumentative'*. Yes, also in private the Dutch like outspoken opinions: you only really get to know someone when you *dis*agree on a subject, don't you? So they use – and are used to – firm statements, which will then be watered down in the ensuing discussion. The pros and cons will be balanced and a common standpoint reached – or, if not, there will be a clear picture of why they disagree. After such a discussion they feel they are much closer to the other person than before, so the next encounter will again be more personal, and so on. The result after several such encounters will be true and lasting friendship. Perhaps this is why some non-Dutch people complain that it's hard for them to make friends with the Dutch. By contrast, the Dutch may complain that it is difficult to make really deep contact with non-Dutch people.

So having opinions (and stating them) is a must, not only at work but also in society as a whole. But in spite of what the non-Dutch call *'strong and intolerant opinions'*, public life as a whole gives the impression of tolerance to all kinds of behaviour.

Looks *'Boy, you've got strange news presenters here. Some of them are really old, others haven't combed their hair for years, it seems. I think they look terrible.'* (My Australian brother who works in television)

Well, in Dutch society content is generally considered more important than external aspects, and people should be free to look the way they want. A Dutch gossip magazine, however, attacked the appearance and way of presentation of one of the older newsreaders. This led others to protest, but it all goes to show that not everyone in Holland is tolerant, or politically correct....

Freedom and non-interference   Society may be divided but parliament and local councils (equally divided) set the overall rules, laid down after lengthy discussion and compromise. The overall effect is that they aren't really any rules for particular groups, rather a cocktail of differing ideas, respected to a greater or lesser degree by all. If people do not agree with a particular general rule, or don't see the need for it, they tend to ignore it, or break it. I have already mentioned tax evasion, bikers' anarchistic behaviour and pushing in queues and crowds. Other examples are far more serious, truly criminal. Sometimes the tolerant approach resulting from compromise is not to the public's liking. Calling it 'soft' and 'ineffective', they may take the law into their own hands. In the last few years, there have been local actions against the establishment of a refugee centre for asylum seekers and self-organised violent protest against real or perceived paedophiles in a particular area, and against drug users' hindrance.

Such people feel that they are defending their own interests, starting from the standpoint of their own sub-cultural norms and values. Significantly, there is a slow rise in the popularity of local-interest political parties, at times quite populist, at the cost of the more traditional ideologically based parties. Intellectuals worry about the general decrease of political interest, demonstrated by lower turnouts at elections.

Taboos   In individual talks with the Dutch few subjects are taboo. Exceptions might be one's income and one's voting behaviour, these being things that most people prefer to keep to themselves. Mentioning high or low *income* spoils the myth of egalitarianism, while the casual question 'who do you vote for?' might be met with an open refusal to answer, since the question may easily be taken as an enquiry about their lifestyle and philosophy.

On national level things are more complicated. From the 1960s on one taboo after the other was broken. Satirical television programmes and certain political groups made jokes about religion, sexuality, the monarchy and other hitherto 'touchy' subjects. At first this often caused scandal, but gradually it became quite normal. But it was 'not done' to make negative comments at jokes about the ethnic minorities – often in under-privileged positions – in a society where underdogs are supposed to be supported. Generally speaking, any *public* remarks on underprivileged people of any kind will be met with some protest, but in more *private* conversations the Dutch are certainly not always politically correct….

One last point: even when critical themselves, many Dutch people may not much appreciate *foreign* criticism of the idio-syncrasies of their social and political system, or the royal family. They will probably conclude that 'outsiders' don't know or under-stand the finer points anyway.

These days, if there is an argument in the streets few people will intervene, either out of respect (at best) or indifference (at worst) for the other norms of those involved. In the first edition I wrote here: 'not so much out of fear'. Unfortunately, this seems to be changing. In recent years several people, just out for the evening, have for no apparent reason been attacked and sometimes killed by young drunks. This 'senseless violence' has caused great protest and concern in society as a whole, but apart from demanding more police vigilance, nobody knows what the solution might be. An unfortunate effect, however, is that more than before people tend to turn their backs on any trouble they come across.

All this freedom, all this non-interference, has other dark sides too, of course, and these are noticed especially by those from countries with strong local and family ties: *'Not everyone is like that* (stand-offish), *but most people are. The way of life here is very sad to me. I can't get used to it, no matter how long I live here. All this strong individualism. Everyone to himself.'* (Cameroon) *'The Dutch have a mind-your-own-business type of life.'* (Tanzania)

The Dutch seek their social contacts mostly within the group they feel to belong to, people who share their norms and values, their tastes and preferences. This may keep them from meeting outsiders, which of course doesn't feel very inviting to foreigners. In public life, they usually mind their own business. Still, people from western countries are sometimes happily surprised: *'Generally speaking, people here are friendly. Not like Paris, where you can live somewhere for five years without knowing the neighbours. Here people sometimes suddenly ring your doorbell to ask whether you would like to come for a glass of wine. In other countries that happens only by previous arrangement, days beforehand.'* (Italy)

Luckily, I hear more positive stories from people with good neighbours or who have met helpful or friendly Dutch people, but I'm afraid the following observation from an Irish woman is just as typical, especially in cities: *'Here you don't just drop in to see a friend, you arrange a meeting and note it in your diary. But every time I do that, I wonder: will I feel like it that day?'* And from another part of the world: *'People here are different, more business-like. I have only once visited a Dutch home, for reasons of work, but never for just a cup of tea.'* (Egypt)

Dutch society leaves you free to live the way you want to live, without much intervention by other people or the authorities. On a summer afternoon at Dutch beaches you may see women sunbathing topless without anyone taking offence. In any town you can see police officers walking past cafés which are exuding an aroma of cannabis. In a survey carried out in 2000, 77% of the Dutch said that they found homosexual relations normal and acceptable, a far higher percentage than in other European countries. In parliament a large majority voted to legalise homosexual marriage and 62% of the Dutch were in favour of this measure, although many don't see the need now that fewer and fewer heterosexual couples are marrying. Childless couples having children by artificial insemination is now commonplace. Amsterdam's Free University, originally founded by Calvinists, now offers psychological and medical support to people wanting a sex change.

Permissive society?   Many foreigners (including visiting journalists) see the Netherlands as a free, tolerant, even permissive, society. Depending on their own standards, they are amazed, pleased or shocked by the open attitudes. Some are outright critical of all this freedom: *'It is shocking for us to see so much nudity on television and on the beaches. I find this a problem with our children.'* (Malaysia). I do understand their problem, but then, Dutch expatriates in Muslim countries are also shocked by some things, which are acceptable there.

Quite often the misunderstanding that 'anything goes' in Holland, that Dutch law is endlessly tolerant, prevails. It doesn't and it isn't – there are limits. Quite a few things may happen out in the open, but this doesn't always mean they are legal. Often they are officially illegal but tolerated in practice. Regarding the above examples, most matters concerning sexuality and nudity are not regulated by Dutch national legislation, since personal freedom is guaranteed in the constitution. Even so, certain kinds of pornography are definitely illegal (which is not the same as non-existent!), municipal councils may allow nudity on beaches but not elsewhere, prostitution may be tolerated in some parts of the city but not in others.

The basic idea behind Dutch legislation in such controversial matters is that they happen anyway, all over the world, whether we like it or not. This being so, the best thing is to try and bring them out into the open and legislate on them, in order to create a generally acceptable and practically applicable framework for dealing with them, a way of combining the ideal (they don't exist) and reality (they do).

Anything goes? In an article on the European football championships held in Holland and Belgium in June 2000, the International Herald Tribune wrote, referring to British and Turkish soccer fans: '... *a strange match of potential nationalist breast-pounding versus a culture of carefully managed permissiveness, the non-confrontational environment here, may be seducing the street-fighting yobbos of European soccer into non-violence. (…)* After describing the non-violent start of the games, it continued with quoting the Dutch Interior Minister: *'Abroad, people think that everything is allowed in Holland. So for us, the championship is a great occasion to show that it isn't. Our police are friendly but forceful.'*

Euthanasia   Dutch consensus usually has an element of 'having your cake and eating it'. Many Dutch laws on issues like these might be translated as: 'No, this is prohibited, unless conditions 1 through 4 are fulfilled' or: 'Yes, this is allowed, but only if criteria a, b and c are met'. Let us take active euthanasia as an example, the medical ending of human life. This unique legal arrangement has come under fierce international criticism, ranging from the Vatican to quite progressive newspapers, comparing the Dutch approach to Nazi policy, calling it 'a culture of death', or even accusing the Dutch of wanting to save money on health care. But the legislation is quite in line with Dutch culture, initially enforced 'bottom-up' by the actions of private citizens who felt their parents and loved ones to be in great need and distress. It is felt that when all is said and done it is not a doctor but the patient who is the master of his/her own life. All the practical and emotional pros and cons were extensively and quite rationally debated in both the media and in parliament. The ensuing law is felt to support and comfort people living out the last days or weeks of their lives in great pain and misery, and it is seen as an acceptable and humane solution to a realistic and urgent demand by people in society. So what exactly is the scope of this law, and how much of a 'no but yes' arrangement is it?

In 2000, after years of recurring debate, the Dutch parliament took a final decision on euthanasia. On both occasions the foreign press announced in sensational ways that euthanasia is now legal under Dutch law. It is not. Euthanasia in the Netherlands is *not* legal as such, parliament decided, but those practising it will not be prosecuted as long as the following five strict conditions are met: (a) the patient him/herself has explicitly and in full possession of his/her faculties expressed the wish to not live under conditions of a disease which (b) two independent doctors verify to be (c) incurable and (d) causing unbearable suffering. Then one of the two doctors may – but is not obliged to against his own will – end the patient's life. Immediately afterwards, this must be (e) reported to the medical authorities – not for legal prosecution but for medical judgement and registration. Needless to say that family doctors, having sworn the Hippocratic oath on medical ethics, will do their utmost to persuade the patient that life can still be lived in a dignified manner. Only if the patient continues to insist that they want to die will the doctor administer the drugs necessary to bring about a painless death.

The 'no but yes' aspect of the law may appear hypocritical, but the majority of Dutch people (with the obvious exception of religious fundamentalists) would deny this. They perceive their legislation and less official arrangements on such subjects as finely tuned to the demands of the complexities of any modern society reflecting and encompassing widely different points of view. Dutch pragmatism also shines through. Concerned about potential abuse, researchers discovered that patients to whom euthanasia was administered would have lived, on average, only two – very unpleasant – weeks longer.

Drugs policy   Drugs are a comparable 'hot' issue, raising foreign eyebrows and certainly causing a good deal of worry among expats with teenage children. Throughout the world Holland is known for its lenient policy on cannabis and marihuana. *'Only the Netherlands has legalised its (*marijuana*) sale in Europe.'* (From the same IHT article

quoted above) *'Dutch drugs policy makes the German drug problem worse'*
(German politician from Bavaria, August 2000)

Besides its reputation as a haven for users of cannabis and
marijuana, in recent years Holland also acquired the reputation of
being a (or even: *the*) major exporter of 'party drugs' such as XTC
(ecstasy). Cannabis, marijuana and XTC are indeed easy to get in
Dutch cities, from coffee shops and street vendors, in discos and at
dance parties, and foreign authorities catch quite a few Dutch smug-
glers. Contrary to what the IHT reports, neither of these, nor any
other drug, is officially legal. But if this is so, how come they are so
easy to get? Why do you never see the police arrest those street
vendors, or go into the coffee shops?

It is not easy to answer this. As with euthanasia, Dutch policy is
confusing to outsiders (and sometimes to insiders too), combining
legal prohibition with turning a blind eye to users in everyday life.
There are some misunderstandings to be cleared in this field.

Internationally known by now, this tolerant policy applies to what
the Dutch call 'soft-drugs'[2], not to cocaine, heroine and other 'hard
drugs'. Individual users of the latter are considered to be medical
cases rather than criminals and are helped whenever possible. But
dealing in hard drugs is illegal and prosecuted, be it that the (under-
staffed) police prefers to concentrate on large-scale dealers. So petty
street vendors are usually ignored, hard to control as they are anyway.

Production or large-scale dealing is not treated mildly. Every year
the police destroy many small ecstasy factories and 'hash plantations',
Dutch customs and excise officers confiscate large quantities of drugs,
be they 'hard' or 'soft', and arrest producers and dealers if they can.
This happens in Dutch ports and at border crossings, but also in the
Caribbean islands called the Netherlands Antilles, officially Dutch,
where there is co-operation with the US authorities in the 'war on
drugs'. But Rotterdam is the world's largest port, the Dutch economy
thrives on foreign trade and those Caribbean islands are almost within
sight of a number of major hard-drug producing countries. So there is
considerable export and transit trade going on over Dutch territory. It
was estimated that in 1999, the illegal export of soft drugs from the
Netherlands amounted to almost $150 million!

When in the mid-1990s a diplomatic row developed between
France and Holland over the issue of drugs, Dutch politicians and
newspapers came up with figures indicating the success of the nation's drugs policy in keeping the number of addicts low, in separating

'soft drugs' from 'hard drugs', etc. A French journalist living in Holland then told a newspaper that drug use in France is considerable at all levels of society, but hushed up. He added: *'The Dutch reduce drugs to numbers, expenses, percentages. It is a materialistic type of consuming. The French are also materialistic but the Dutch are that in a harder way, without any wrapping. (...) Dutchmen look at things in life in their full nakedness, they see themselves with all their mistakes. The French see themselves less sharply, they keep more of a distance, they soften things and embellish them.'*

Although since then French-Dutch debate and even police co-operation on the issue has resulted in a better understanding of the mutual viewpoints, it may still be worth looking at the quote, because it demonstrates a crucial cultural difference between 'Germanic' Holland and 'Latin' France. Remember the term 'Newtonian'? Indeed, the Dutch prefer to face reality, even when it's not pleasant to look at, and totally forbidden fruits may be more attractive than half-legal ones. Whether it's soft drugs, prostitution or euthanasia, Dutch authorities try to limit the problem by actively discouraging the practice, while not prosecuting those engaging in them.

This ambivalent and at times paradoxical policy is described in Dutch with the word *gedogen*, allowing. Unusual measures and experiments to find a balance have been tried, some have been more successful than others, some more accepted by the public than others. The (in)famous 'coffee shops' that may sell limited quantities of soft drugs only, the free testing of XTC pills at discos and house parties, and the relief centre for hard drug users in a Rotterdam church, are a few examples.

Dutch law is strict on hard drugs, but users (unlike dealers!) are perceived as pitiful creatures, more victims of circumstances than criminals. People may not like to have them around, but the general idea is that when all is said and done they are human beings, so they should be tolerated and helped. In August 2000, the Burgomaster of Amsterdam asked people to stop offering drug addicts food and shelter, because that makes it more difficult for the authorities to fight the problem. The police, welfare organisations, social workers, churches etc. are working together to help drug users and at the same time to limit the spread of the use of drugs. Nonetheless, people from other cultures are often shocked by the openness of the coffee shops and soft drug use.

Needless to say, criminals try to take advantage of this 'softly, softly' approach. With drug-related crime rising and public disturbance increasing in certain urban areas, resistance to this policy is growing. Now in the Netherlands itself people are beginning to question whether perhaps the whole approach doesn't work after all and should be revised, certainly in the light of growing European unity and interaction. The German politician's remark, if true, is just one more piece of evidence.

Nonetheless, the generally humane approach to the drug *users* problem is praised at international conferences on the issue, and most Dutch people are rather proud of this. They see it, basically, as a just system, not flawless, but the best available, well considered, the outcome of the democratic process and precious compromise.

Tobacco and tolerance   Far more widespread than any soft or hard drug use is smoking cigarettes and *shag* (self-rolled cigarettes). Foreigners were already complaining about this 350 years ago, as they travelled through Holland by public transport(!), in covered boats that sailed between cities at fixed hours. Some things never really change, the Dutch still smoke a great deal, and foreigners[3] still complain about it, as do those Dutch people who don't smoke. The statistics have changed, however. In 1960, 90% of all Dutch adult males smoked, and 30% of all females. In 1998, only 39% of all men smoked, although among women the figure was still the same 30%.[4] Generally speaking, the percentage of smokers rises as one goes down the social ladder, but also quite a few people in intellectual and artistic circles still smoke.

Anti-tobacco groups accuse the government of a half-hearted policy, indicating that taxes on tobacco put a great deal of money in the nation's coffers. Smoking is forbidden in most companies, in all public buildings and in most public transport, but not, to the dismay of many visitors to our shores, in restaurants and cafés. Companies may still allow smoking in special places and one-person offices, and in public places you see people ignoring the No-Smoking signs. Up until now only one legal action has been taken by someone to secure a smoke-free work environment. The woman won her case, but her colleagues regarded her as 'intolerant' and 'fanatic' and she was forced to leave her job. (The affair led to some public discussion on tolerance...)

If you can't stand the smoke in places where smoking is allowed, the best you can probably do is to ask the smokers, in a friendly manner, if they would mind, etc. Especially with strangers, any haughty or impatient behaviour is likely to be met with disdain, opposition or perhaps with strong words. Tolerance is not always a two-sided thing....

The social benefits system The crucial role of the social benefit system has come up several times in this book. Let's take a closer look at its roots. First, an observation: *'In a society (like the Dutch) where people can easily get social benefits, even for an unlimited period, indifference will prevail. (...) This seems to me unfavourable, because in fact it means there is too little development in such a society. I also get irritated about the ease with which people on benefits can work 'black'. But I must admit that occasionally I do something black too. It is so tempting, you know.'* (USA) Aha!

Obviously, The Dutch system of social benefits matches old-time Christian attitudes towards the weak in society, but it evolved through state institutions rather than through religious ones. It can be seen as 'mechanical solidarity', organised by and through the state, replacing the old-time 'organic solidarity' within families and church communities, between friends and neighbours. But even in the cities some of the latter also remains, small-scale and unpublicised.

With the industrial revolution (after 1880 in Holland) growing state influence and the emancipation of the working classes resulted in protective laws against 'capitalist exploitation'. First, child labour was forbidden (1884). Soon after, restrictions were put on working hours, and basic assistance was organised for sick or injured workers. More and more categories of people were covered by protective laws. At first only employees of government and private companies were involved. But as a result of the severe economic crisis in the 1930s that brought unemployment and poverty to millions, also people outside the workforce were included, albeit under strict conditions.

After the enormous damage caused in the Second World War had been repaired, it was felt necessary to do something to improve the lot of the weaker groups in society. A law passed in 1956 guaranteed a state pension for everyone over the age of 65. In the 1960s more social benefits were established, especially under the Labour dominated government of the early 1970s; remember the WAO case.

During those years the prevailing idea was that society is a human construction that could be perfected if people only tried hard enough. Anyone who faced problems, whether through unemployment, drugs or for some other reason, was considered to be a victim of circumstances beyond their control, and deserving of other people's attention and support. Welfare organisations sprang up for all kinds of people, paid for by government subsidies financed by increasingly high taxation.

In the 1990s the social climate changed and hardened. Society has individualised and there is less emphasis on egalitarianism. There is more praise for 'winners' and less compassion for 'losers'. They, too, should work for their money, and there is increasing irritation about benefit abuse. It is much appreciated that homeless people now sell magazines at supermarket exits. Since 1980 it is also said that the whole expensive system is economically damaging to the country, so various administrations have worked on reducing it, by economising, restricting the quantity and quality of benefits, bringing down taxation, privatising insurances, etc. Nowadays the younger generations find it quite normal to make additional private arrangements to cover any future mishap, for old age, and the like. The tax system introduced in 2001 will encourage still more individual responsibility. Yet even now, a subsidised government programme helps less well-educated unemployed people to get jobs such as public transport controllers or city wardens, intended to have a positive influence on safety and public order on the streets. But saying you have such a 'Melkert'-job (named after the politician who dreamed up the idea) is akin to admitting you're under-skilled and difficult to employ.

Yet, in spite of the hardening of official policy regarding social benefits, Dutch society will probably continue to be based on some form of collective responsibility for the well-being of fellow citizens for a long time to come. Quite a few Dutch organisations are beginning to comment that government policy is too much focussed on economic issues and not on social well-being.

With European integration the Dutch system is coming under increasing pressure from other countries, but when foreign critics cannot convince the Dutch of the superiority of their own approach, they dig their heels in. Criticism is fine, but the argumentation should be sound, unemotional, based solidly on facts. If it isn't, the Dutch defend their views vigorously, and it becomes a matter of national pride.

1. *American Cultural Patterns*, E.C. Stewart & M.J. Bennett, 1991, The Intercultural Press, Maine.
2. A term not recognised in many other countries.
3. Depending very much on where they come from, I notice, having been a smoker myself.
4. Figures by Stivoro, an organisation against smoking.

Chapter 9

THE INTERNATIONAL OUTLOOK

'He who wants to be someone, should not sit still, but put to sea'
(old Dutch saying)

Dutch traders were already sailing the seas some 700 years ago. Now, more than ever before, the Dutch are trading and doing business with countries in every corner of the world.

The Dutch like going places, either for business or for pleasure. Their small country is home to a disproportionate number of multi-national companies and banks operating worldwide and has vast investments on every continent. For example, the Netherlands is the second highest foreign investor in the USA, and in the year 2000 was ranked third in the world in the field of international take-overs.[1] Many Dutch firms export a large part of what they produce, making this tiny country the world's eighth largest trading nation, while Dutch trucking and shipping firms are the great freight carriers of Europe. All in all, more than 200,000 Dutch people – not counting those who have officially emigrated – work abroad in countries ranging from neighbouring Germany to far away Papua New Guinea, although it must be admitted that companies, due to dual careers, are now having problems finding people willing to give up their life at home for an international job with uncertain career prospects.

With its open economy, the Netherlands was among the original founders of the European Union. It is still strongly advocating further integration and is even willing to give up certain national symbols in order to achieve it.

People from other countries cannot fail to notice this international attitude: *'I don't know any other country that is so cosmopolitan, so receptive to foreign influences as Holland. It is a friendly, open country where a foreigner feels at ease immediately.'* (Switzerland). And from Japan: *'Dutch people are very open-minded. For instance, in shops one sees a lot of Chinese and Japanese food. It must also be because you speak English so well.'*

Think globally, act locally. More and more Dutch firms are becoming aware of the necessity of adapting their products, their advertising and the behaviour of their representatives in order to meet the standards and the requirements of local markets. In response to these needs governmental and business organisations in the Netherlands provide valuable export information; language institutes cater also for the business world and it is not difficult to find literature and statistics on even the remotest countries.

None of this is new, it is merely the present state of an old tradition. As long ago as the 15th century the Dutch were shipping merchandise between the Baltic and Portugal. In the wake of the 16th-century Spanish and Portuguese discoveries overseas, the Dutch trading empire expanded to Africa and the Americas, to the Arctic Ocean, to Ceylon and Indonesia, even to isolationist Japan, where the Dutch held a trade monopoly for centuries.

It was the Dutch who discovered Australia, and who founded New York (under its original name of New Amsterdam) and Cape Town. All over the world remains of this Dutch trading empire can be found – in physical remains, in geographical names, in words absorbed into local languages and in shipping terminology.

In the 17th century, the so-called 'Golden Age', many foreign visitors came to study the achievements of the very cosmopolitan Dutch republic. Two famous admirers were Czar Peter the Great, who came here in search of the technology to modernise his navy, and the French philosopher Descartes, who studied and published in Holland.

People prosecuted for their religion in their own country, such as the French Huguenots and the Jews of Spain and Portugal, sought refuge in the Netherlands. The English Pilgrim Fathers found shelter in Holland for some time before they set sail for America. All these visitors and immigrants added to the international orientation of the republic.

At home the Dutch were smug, thrifty and careful, but overseas they found challenge and adventure. In the 19th and early 20th centuries colonialism was the outlet for adventurous Dutchmen, while nowadays it is international business and development work that offer wider horizons.

The world: a potential market – and a holiday destination
To the Dutch the world has always been a potential market, and to be successful you must know your market well. Dutch schools spend more teaching hours on foreign languages than any other European nation, and foreign programmes on Dutch television – and there are

plenty of them – are broadcast in the original language, with sub-titling. World geography is taught in all schools and foreign news is reported in depth in the Dutch media. Many Dutch people are also well informed on foreign events in non-commercial ways, through personal contacts and special interest groups such as Greenpeace, Amnesty International or the Foster Parents Plan, which have far more members in the Netherlands than in surrounding countries. In an earlier chapter I mentioned the large amounts of money the Dutch donate to campaigns for victims of disasters worldwide. One effect may be that many people develop a rather gloomy outlook on the international scene: *'Many Dutchmen know much more about Africa and my country than I expected. Unfortunately it was mostly the negative aspects.'* (Nigeria)

On more official levels, the Dutch government is very keen to play a leading global role, supporting international collaboration not only in the European Union, but also in NATO and various UN peace missions. It is proud to be the home of the International Court of Justice (where the current Yugoslavia war crime tribunal is being held), and of having provided the first President of the European bank, Wim Duisenberg. Several Dutch diplomats are internationally active in the field of human rights, not always in the full glare of publicity, while in other fields international humanitarian or environmental organisations virtually always have Dutch executives. It isn't difficult to see that this is a modern version of old-time religious social involvement.

At the same time, however, we should not overlook the fact that this country is also the world's sixth largest arms exporter, and one of the world's largest importers of tropical hardwoods!

Lots of leisure time   *'This is ridiculous, Holland is locked up in summer, the whole economy comes to a standstill and you can't reach anyone!'* (USA) Yes, and the same is true for two weeks around Christmas and New Year.

Let's first look at the official labour arrangements concerning holidays, and then how people like to spend them.

People with a full-time job usually have 25 days – five weeks – paid holiday a year. In some branches there may be a limit to the number of days they can take at one time, and of course parents must take their children's school holidays into account, but quite a few people can, and do, take three or four weeks off in summer, saving the rest for Christmas or perhaps a week's skiing holiday. For people covered by a CAO agreement, a premium is withheld from their salary during the year. This is reimbursed as 'holiday money', together with their May salary payment. Even people on social benefit receive an extra payment for a holiday!

'I was told that all construction workers here have to go on holiday at the same time. Why on earth is that?' (Switzerland). The answer is because in the construction industry it is considered more efficient to close down building sites completely for a few weeks than to work throughout summer with anything up to a third of the workers absent at any given time. But most people follow the rhythm set by the school holidays (the country is divided into three zones, each zone having a different holiday period). Most people make individual arrangements in consultation with their immediate boss and their colleagues.

On top of their regular holidays, employees under a CAO-regulated contract may have as many as 13 so-called ATV (Labour Time Reduction) days. This scheme was included in the 1982 agreement, which triggered the 'polder model'. In those days there was very high unemployment and in return for the trade unions agreeing to 'freeze' salaries[2] employers agreed to have people with full-time jobs work 38 hours a week instead of 40, for the same salary. This gave workers a day off every four weeks – their 13 ATV-days a year. It was hoped the accumulated millions of hours of 'work' would create new employment. In the end, as the global economy began to improve, this scheme did help to create more jobs.

So, theoretically, people on full-time contracts can enjoy 38 days paid holiday a year, apart from weekends and bank holidays. Combined with the high degree of part-time work, this makes the Netherlands the country with the lowest number of hours worked per person per year, leading – as we have seen – people from other countries to comment that it is a relaxed country, and even to wonder whether the Dutch are a lazy nation.

This statistic still holds good when we take into account the moderation in the 1990s. As the labour market got tighter due to the success of the polder model, employers started wanting people to go back to working longer hours. So nowadays, to degrees which vary per branch and per company, people can 'sell' this time back to the boss. They can also save up the days and use them later for 'sabbaticals' or for early retirement.

Employers themselves, and people with jobs higher than (or outside) CAO-levels, don't have ATV days, of course. But most of them still have – and take – far longer holidays than their colleagues in other countries. The only real exceptions may be farmers, people in very small companies, or the self-employed.

And now: travel! So how do people spend all this free time? The Dutch love to travel. The Saturday newspapers are full of travel advertisements, and one is liable to encounter Dutch tourists and backpackers in the most remote countries. (But even adventure should be well-prepared, as an American noticed: *'You guys always prepare your trips by reading a million guide books. We Americans don't do that'*). Even at home, the Dutch are open to foreign influence as well, ranging from food to literature and music.

The Dutch like 'going places'. And they have the time and money to do it. Some twenty years ago the trend was set with 2 or 3-week holidays in Mediterranean beach resorts. This type of holiday is still very popular today. People with more money and no children may want something more adventurous. You'll find Dutch people everywhere on earth! But they remain Dutch: a survey published in 2000 revealed that the Dutch spend about half as much money per holiday than other Europeans do. And to my surprise a Dutch coach driver just recently told me that on his trips to Spain he indeed still sees quite a few Dutch people with caravans full of their own food. Yet in another survey it was found that people expected to spend on average some 2,000 euro on their holidays in 2001, 10% more than the previous year. With more work pressure many people, especially those without children, now prefer to make several short trips a year. But in the end, all these people return to the comfort and the snugness of the Netherlands.

Anti-chauvinism With all the country's international renown and economic power one would think the Dutch would be awfully proud of their country. But they don't really seem to be, certainly when talking about it among themselves. They love their country dearly, of course, but compared to many other nations, national pride is not really well developed (...yet, perhaps we should say. Things seem to be changing, see below).

Generally speaking, the Dutch public does not seem to be particularly aware of their country's renown or power, and many people who are seem to take it more or less for granted, assuming the rest of the world is just as internationally minded.

'There should be more admiration for the good and beautiful things of Holland. This is such a small country and yet there are world personalities in the fields of art, literature, sports, film. Why aren't they proud of it, I am! The Dutch anti-chauvinism shocks and irritates me tremendously.' (Argentine)

Although in recent years admiration for world champions and international stars has greatly increased, there is more than a grain of truth in the Argentinean's observation. In the Netherlands, pride in one's own nation and culture have rarely been strongly developed or greatly stimulated by government, schools or the media. Only in the face of foreign animosity has this been different – for example during the Nazi occupation. Many people kept a national flag hidden away, were moved to tears by the voice of the Queen broadcasting from her London exile, and secretly wore orange to express their (forbidden) royalist sympathies. But after the war identification with one's own peer group took over again.

Nowadays, many people don't even know the words of the national anthem[3] and the flag is not that much honoured anymore: you may see cafés unceremoniously decorate their premises with it and families flying it at private celebrations of birthdays or passed exams.

As a result, other nations' displays of nationalism are felt to be slightly ridiculous or even outright irritating. The Dutch distrust countries in which the head-of-state's portrait hangs everywhere, where street slogans boast of national achievements, where school children are forced to sing national anthems or perform flag ceremonies.

Listening to Dutch people grumbling about the imperfections of their society, one might be tempted to think that they don't love their country. However, referring to the Argentinean's irritations with 'Dutch anti-chauvinism', it is important to remember that in Dutch culture criticism is an indirect expression of concern or appreciation. So complaining about society or talking critically about certain conditions means that people care. People from other countries may not understand this: *'The Netherlands is constantly occupied with making itself smaller than it really is. That is the real 'hollanditis', a virus that has spread quite widely and that affects people in the street, the professor at university and the politician. (....) Self-scoffing is an often-practised sport. The economy is the only field in which the Netherlands doesn't suffer from an inferiority-complex.'* (France)

I would certainly include football in this last sentence, but it is true that the Dutch don't seem to be proud of themselves. (Some might even say that this book is just another piece of evidence to support this idea...)

Public negligence of official culture   Yet the Dutch do love their country. They are fond of its nature, proud of its waterworks, they care for its wildlife, its old city centres, its windmills. Foreign eyebrow raising has also made them more aware and proud of national accomplishments such as the 'polder model', the welfare state and the large degree of political and personal freedom. But it is a rather rational kind of love, practical things rather than symbols. Millions are spent on restoring old houses and castles and on saving vulnerable patches of woodland or swamp, and the money certainly doesn't only come from the government. Because these examples are visible, foreigners used to more symbolic or verbal expressions of nationalism may well not see them as expressions of patriotism.

'Hungarians have an emotional bonding to their language. How come the Dutch awareness of language and history is so weak?' I think one answer to this question can be found in the Dutch preference for achieved (as opposed to ascribed) status. It's not so much the things our ancestors, our historical heroes, did that count. No, what is important, what we can really be proud of, is our own efforts, what we have accomplished ourselves in this day and age. So new things are more a source of pride than old things. We don't dismiss the old, but neither do we have a very strong attachment to it. We see our historical heritage largely as a pleasant background to present-day accomplishments. One result is that we are more proud of speaking foreign languages than we are of mastering our own. Many people are sloppy in their Dutch – why bother using a dictionary when the computer has a spelling checker programme? And many shrug their shoulders at other people's linguistic mistakes (if they notice them at all...).

To most Dutch people the Dutch language is a 'home, garden and kitchen'-thing, an expression used to indicate its everyday, unspectacular character. Many Dutch people love doing crosswords, many enjoy reading, but few become emotional about the qualities or the unique character of the language. Foreign cynics may suggest that perhaps this is because it doesn't have any qualities. Well, you may not like the throaty sound of the Dutch G, but there *is* poetry, world class literature and quite a few excellent songs in Dutch, as well as plenty of good jokes and puns.

Foreigners speaking Dutch   The casual attitude the Dutch have to their language may also explain why foreigners learning to speak Dutch are looked upon with (happy) surprise, but not taken very seriously: *'They are very supportive of beginners' Dutch'*, said someone on my course. But it would appear he was the exception that proves the rule, because most Dutch people prefer to switch to English rather than exercise the patience to wait for the slow beginner's answer. Many expatriates practising their newly acquired Dutch get frustrated, like this Englishman: *'It is convenient of course that everyone speaks English, but they even answer me in English when I want to use my Dutch. How do they expect me to learn it if they don't give me the chance to practice?'* May I pass on to the reader one Italian's solution to this problem: *'When they answer me in English, I pretend that besides some Dutch I only speak Italian!'*

But even in this field things seem to be changing: some people on my courses complain that all meetings at their office are in Dutch. *'There is little sympathy for non-Dutch speakers. They expect you to learn Dutch yesterday!'* (Australia) Most likely this refers to a work environment where non-managerial staff also participate in meetings, because among Dutch managers this would not generally be the case. But it may also be a side effect of increasing public impatience about the frequently slow integration of immigrants into Dutch society.

A few more things should be said about the use of English in the Netherlands. On my courses some newcomers complain: *'In shops, everything is in Dutch'*, or: *'Information, magazines and books are mostly in Dutch'*, but in my view these people obviously don't know what it's like in other countries. The use of English in the Netherlands – in education, in business, in advertising, in everyday life – is increasing at a faster rate than it is in Germany, Belgium or France. When formerly publicly-owned companies are privatised they are likely to replace their old Dutch name by a 'sexy' English one, much to the chagrin of the older generation.

It is all intended to evoke an image of cosmopolitanism, of global culture. For example, in Dutch language job advertisements English job titles – such as *chief technology officer, human resources director, key account retail manager, strategic tariffing manager, recruitment consultants, legal advisor employee benefits* – for which there are perfectly good Dutch equivalents, are frequently used.

After decades of exposure to American and English pop music and years of hard-to-translate computer terminology, using English terms while speaking Dutch has become common practice, although it is regretted by some. Though the home market is small the world market is enormous and the Dutch businessman uses English to give his company a more international image, hoping this will result in greater sales of their products.

An official government policy against this, like the French objections to 'Franglais', is unlikely to come about. The use of English is also growing in education. Students and academics reading books and articles in English, German *and* French is quite an old tradition here. Now, increasingly, they are being stimulated to *write* in English, to strengthen the links between Dutch academia and the dominant Anglophone world. At the same time, fewer and fewer people speak good French and German. In a test carried out by a language institute a few years ago the telephone operators of several companies became so nervous when called by a French-speaking 'customer' that they simply broke off the connection! And German business people in Holland now often speak English, or even Dutch, to their counterparts, but that may be their own choice. *'Sometimes they are reserved about Germans, but if you try to speak Dutch it gets better.'*

National pride? *'Secretly the Dutch cherish everything that can make a small country seem large: the Delta works, the Rotterdam harbour, their world class football. But they say: 'We're just a small country''* (France)

Some countries loudly trumpet their cultural heritage, not only abroad, for tourist promotion, but also to their own citizens, in schools and the media, to raise awareness and national pride. This doesn't happen much in Holland, one reason being the sensitivities of a multicultural society (see chapter 11). The Dutch school system tries to prepare students for today's society and for their careers, emphasising personal development and social participation, rather than giving them facts and figures about culture and history. In this view, national chauvinism would be out of place in a united Europe and in a world striving for peace and justice for all. A perhaps-negative effect of this approach: a few years ago members of the Dutch Parliament were tested on their knowledge of national history. Most of them failed!

So Dutch upbringing and education produce assertive citizens, but citizens with a remarkable lack of pride in their own culture. Achievements in the fields of literature and the arts are no great source of pride to most Dutch people. It comes as somewhat of a surprise to them to realise that nowadays translated Dutch literature is very successful abroad.

The country's rich past and present are taken for granted to a large extent. Although the intellectual elite organises successful exhibitions at home and abroad, the general Dutch public is not particularly interested in the international prestige of the Dutch arts. Many people are only familiar with the names of painters, composers, designers, inventors and scholars from the 15th century to the present day because they have streets named after them. Dutch business people do not always fully appreciate or make use of the country's good image in fields such as the arts and waterworks technology. Nor are they impressed if foreigners use *their* national glories to promote their business. The Dutch government does not spend very much money publicising Dutch culture abroad. Much more is spent promoting export and trade. Some years ago it took pressure from the much more language-conscious Flemish before subsidies were provided for the promotion of Dutch literature at the famous Frankfurt Book Fair in Germany. In 2000, only protest from intellectual circles prevented the government from scrapping the subsidy for a British university's Dutch language and literature department.

Nationalism after all?   Contrary to the public negligence of *official* culture, but consistent with their 'act normal'-attitude, the Dutch can be quite chauvinistic when it comes to more mundane achievements. *'Come on, what are you saying? The Dutch are super-nationalists! Look at those crowds in orange! We even saw shops full of orange decorations, orange cakes, orange custard!'* (Britain). With a bit of luck, if that's the right word, one may indeed encounter celebrating crowds of youngsters waving the national flag, wearing bizarre orange-coloured outfits and wigs, shouting (for once) 'Holland, Holland!' They are sure to be celebrating a national football victory. Sports, football in particular, bring out stronger nationalistic feelings in the Dutch than probably any other event, and over recent years this was stirred up by extensive – and increasingly commercial – media coverage. During international championships, many cars drive around with orange decorations, shops sell orange-coloured food, while fan-club cafés and private houses are covered in flags and orange banners. When Holland played in the 2000 European Cup one man even dyed the grass in his front garden orange.

Perhaps this illustrates something new in Dutch society: increasing nationalism, but of a kind not fuelled by the state or the government. Dutch media analyse what they call 'the Orange-mania' more as an expression of a kind of tribal collectivism than as an outburst of nationalism. As mentioned in the introduction, European unification seems to be leading to increasing national self-awareness all over the continent. When they look closer at their European partners people start thinking: do I want that, what have we got to offer, what have we got to lose? In some cases it may also be a reaction to the presence of foreign minorities.

Being a small country with an important economy, the Netherlands sees itself either the 'largest of the small' in Europe, or the 'smallest of the large'. Neither seems to work very well. The large countries just see it as small, full stop. Some years ago, there was a debate in the Dutch government and media about the country's position in Europe and in the world. Should it turn away from the Atlantic and take a closer look at Germany and beyond? Should it line up with Belgium and Luxembourg, to be better heard as a collective? Should it go on contributing soldiers and money for UN peacekeeping actions in far-away countries? As things stand at the moment the Netherlands remains firmly rooted in the European Union and the world community, with an open eye to all sides, balancing the commercial interests of the economy with the humane ideals of peace, development and equal opportunities for people everywhere.

At least this is the official government position. In the meantime, the Dutch public sees the world as a holiday destination, while the Dutch business world sees it as a huge potential market. To exploit it to the full people read and study, learn other languages and take cultural preparation courses.

1. Spending some 21 billion euro on this, sharing the third place with Switzerland.
2. Implying: no wage rises higher than inflation.
3. Recently, T-shirts with the words of the first verse of the *Wilhelmus* (the Dutch national anthem) were sold to football fans and acted as 'song sheets' for people standing behind them at international matches.

Chapter 10

ON GENDER AND GENERATIONS

Vrouwenvakschool Informatica Amsterdam,
Wodanstraat 1/3, 1076 CC
('Women's vocational training for IT',
as listed in the 2000 Amsterdam telephone directory)

So far we have discussed the 'main stream' Dutch business world – the culture of male, white Dutch most of whom live and work in the Randstad. But only half the population of the country is male, more than half lives outside the Randstad area and many people in the Netherlands are not white. It is time to moderate the general picture painted in the previous chapters.

Women in Dutch society   When you work in the Netherlands you will encounter women everywhere and at all times – but not often in managerial positions. Of course there are exceptions, but usually the women one meets in business are at the mid-level and in administrative jobs. Among men, 21% of employees hold a management post of some description, while among women this is only 5%. As far as government employees are concerned the situation is not that much better. Only in health care, education and other traditionally 'female' jobs, are women over-represented, yet even in these branches there are more men than women at managerial levels. *'If I had known about the position of working women, I would never have come to Holland.'* (Hungary).

In 1996, the United Nations Development Programme rated the Netherlands eleventh in the world in the field of women's education and their position in society; while the country's other 'human development' indicators were among the very best of the world (fourth). Although the difference has almost disappeared, fewer women than men still undertake higher education, and when they do they generally study for a shorter time and mostly take subjects in the fields of social studies, health care, education and literature. Working women produce only a quarter of the Dutch national income. There are also fewer female university professors than in other western and non-western countries. On a brighter note, Holland ranked seventh in the world as far as the political power of women is concerned.[1]

Women at work   Up until just a few decades ago, women's participation in the Dutch labour market was low (1981: 30%). So, too, were their incomes, and their legal status was downright old-fashioned. Although the legal aspects have much improved (partly under European pressure), even today women's participation in the job market, at 51%, is merely average compared with the other EU member states. And most of these jobs (68%) are part-time. If one considers *married* women, the figure is still lower. On average, Dutch women are paid only 77% of their male colleagues' hourly salaries, which is actually a little above the world average. (Compare: USA 75%, Australia 91%, Britain 70%, Bangladesh 42%). This male/ female difference no longer springs from any legal discrimination. It reflects the average Dutch working woman's younger age and her shorter work experience or – if she is older – her outdated job experience due to career interruptions for child raising. But the result of all these factors taken together is that the average income of 35-year old Dutch women is just 16,000 euro, only half that of their male counterparts.

Most working women in the Netherlands are either fairly young[2] or, if not, preferred to concentrate on their career rather than give it up to have children. The latter implies that these are mostly better-educated women. Especially women between the ages of 25 and 35 run the risk of burnout and stress. It is estimated that women in this age group are four times more likely to receive 'WAO' benefit (for people unfit to work) than their male colleagues in the same age group. The causes of this are not all completely clear yet, but it partly has to do with the kind of work women do. Many of them work in health care, which is not an easy job, either emotionally or physically. Both in this sector and in other strongly 'female' sectors of the economy, pay is relatively low, there is a great deal of psychological pressure and career prospects are poor. All these factors also affect job satisfaction. Researchers say that women might also be more sensitive to an unpleasant working atmosphere and therefore likely to give up their job sooner than men. A background role may be played by the fact that many such women have part-time jobs, and there may be another full income in their household. It has also been suggested that women may have a harder struggle to be taken seriously in a still male dominated economy, so they may have to work too hard to prove themselves. A 'glass ceiling' is certainly still present in quite a number of Dutch companies.

The relatively low labour participation of women is not exactly in line with Holland's generally progressive image. Dutch observers cite various reasons. Virtually all point to poor childcare facilities, but since these facilities are improving year by year there must be more to the problem than that. Until two decades ago most women did not work outside their homes which means that the concept of child day-care facilities is relatively new. As the authorities impose strict hygienic, pedagogic and safety standards, it is difficult to start such centres as a private initiative. The official ones, run by organisations and companies, are therefore limited in number and often over-booked, with waiting lists. While this is still a major hindrance, it also reflects the fact that Dutch family life (in the sense of the nuclear family) is quite strong. It may be useful to take a closer look at it.

Individualists? How observers experience Dutch family life depends very much on their own cultural backgrounds. People notice how parents and children eat together and enjoy their leisure time, and it is not only Americans who tell me they are impressed with the Dutch *family orientation*. But people from tropical countries, seeing old people going into homes and hearing about young people ignoring their parents, often comment on the Dutch as being *strong individualists*, or even *cold*. In an international perspective, the Dutch indeed rank among the more individualistic nations, but less so than the Americans. They also have a collectivist side, or perhaps the term 'particularistic' is more appropriate: they tend to cling to their peer-group.

Perhaps not every week, but still on a regular basis, most people have get-togethers either at home or out somewhere, with relatives, friends or neighbours, people who tend to have similar incomes, education and life-style. Such contacts are often life-long, even when people move away from the neighbourhood. Although eating will often be involved, the shared activity, the talking and laughing, is perhaps more important than the meal itself. The Dutch word used for such occasions is *gezellig*, meaning snug and sociable but also implying a certain informal 'in-group' feeling. The word *gezellig* also implicitly refers to things like coffee, cake, a certain arrangement of furniture and room decorations, all contributing to this feeling of 'us-ness', us here in our little box, as opposed to them out there.

'Borrel' In a way, companies and organisations can also be seen as families. Although the social bonds are far more limited than in, for example, Japanese companies, the Dutch also try to create a sense of togetherness at work. Especially people at assistant-levels appreciate a good atmosphere in their depart-ment and Dutch employers may have to limit attempts at making their place of work look *gezellig* with family photos and pot plants. Among close colleagues the need for a group-culture may extend to joint lunches at one table, to out-of-work contacts or outings. Birthdays are celebrated by offering colleagues coffee

and cake. Management may throw an after-hours party – for everyone – on occasions such as a colleague leaving to take up another job or retiring, to celebrate good results, or to mark festivities such as Christmas and New Year. The Dutch word for this is *borrel*, which basically means a 'stiff drink', but it is also used to mean a 'sociable gathering' where, of course, other drinks (and snacks) are available, too. Such parties are good times for in-company networking and for demonstrating who you are on a more personal level. It is a wise policy for foreign employees to attend such occasions because they offer an opportunity to build social contacts with their Dutch colleagues.

Coming back on the nuclear family, many people prefer to raise their kids themselves rather than hire other people to do so. *'They seem to have a very intense family life, and a very active social life.'* (Britain) Until the children are about 16 years of age, most families dine together, go out together and go on holiday together. With the possible exception of people living in the larger cities and the higher income groups, Dutch society in general is still quite strongly geared to family life, and many foreigners find the country positively oriented to children. (Given this general pattern, the Dutch don't have a concept such as 'Quality Time', although the phenomenon of children left in day-care centres, or with au pairs and babysitters, is on the rise in circles of young ambitious couples.) Yet only 19% of Dutch are of the opinion that man/woman roles should be traditional. Only Scandinavian countries are less traditional in this respect.

But family life is rather restricted to the 'nuclear family',[3] which strikes people from other cultures: *'I find it strange that the concept of family here has such a limited meaning. Family here, that is Dad, Mum, brother, sister, sometimes Grandpa and Grandma, but that's it.'* (Cameroon) Even elsewhere in Europe this is apparently different: *'The Dutch have lost the contact between the generations. You never see a grandmother here living with her daughter or son. older people are put away somewhere, there is no family feeling anymore.'* (Ireland) It must be added that Ireland is perhaps one of the more traditional EU countries, but, indeed, it is true that Dutch grandparents usually live elsewhere (see below), and are not often involved in childcare.

Housewives   Until the 1970s, housewives were assumed to have time to do their shopping in the daytime, and this still has its effects in society. Government organisations' opening hours are often from 9 to 5; shopping hours are mostly from 5 to 6. The same is true for repair people visiting your house. This makes foreigners complain that they cannot handle the required bureaucratic procedures or even spend their money: everything is open when they are working but closed when they are not! Quite a few Dutchmen don't see the point, but most people are happy that in 1996 legal restrictions were relaxed and many shops and supermarkets are now open until 9 or 10 in the evening. At first, a majority said that they did not care for longer opening hours, but now, some years later, evening shopping is a success, accounting for 11% of all sales. Some municipal authorities also introduced other opening hours. Customers are mostly hard-working urban youngsters who don't yet have a regular family life, for outside the larger cities, virtually all shops still close at 6pm, to the annoyance of both people from the US and from non-western countries, who are all used to all-day shopping.

The editor of a leading women's magazine gave an another interesting but hard-to-prove view. According to her, Dutch women are quite content to be housewives because after centuries of women running the household in the absence of their sea-faring husbands that position has a higher status in Holland than it does in other countries. Housewives were not only managers of the family but also of the farm or the shop, responsible for the household budget!

A perhaps more plausible explanation can be found in the Dutch tax system. Dutch taxes are not only high but also 'progressive', meaning that the higher the income, the higher the tax percentage. So, unless a couple explicitly states that they want their incomes to be taxed separately, any additional income will be taxed at the higher level. Needless to say this doesn't encourage married women to find a job.

Most working *married* women work part-time, only one in seven having a full-time job, one of the lowest percentages of Europe. One can look at this phenomenon in two ways: negatively, in the sense that they are unable to find a full-time job, or positively, in the sense that they deliberately choose to devote more time to their family. In 1997 a survey found that 70% of working women were content with the number of hours they worked, and that 15% would prefer to work fewer hours.

Also 8% of *men* work part-time. The Dutch labour market has the highest percentage of part-time jobs in the western world (39%). This is made possible because part-timers also have high wages and relatively good job security, although a disadvantage of part time working is that generally it is not too good for one's career. Some years ago the Dutch Parliament almost accepted the legal right to work part-time, much to the dislike of those employers who find it difficult to accommodate such employees in the work process. Employers feel the same about another recurrent trade union hobby-horse: the four-days-a-week job. With present labour shortages in many sectors this is unlikely to become official, but it already exists on a more individual basis: some workers, especially senior people, have successfully negotiated a working week consisting of four 9-hour days. Luckily for the employers, part-time workers are still the exception. The *average* worker in Holland is still a married man whose wife has a part-time job. Yet, in the larger cities, a different impression might emerge. One will see plenty of working women, shops full of customers during evening opening hours, and youngsters eating by themselves at fast food outlets.

Double earners and living together   Among the younger generation, especially in the cities, the phenomenon the Dutch call 'double earners' – two people in one household having a full or part-time paid job – is widespread. After years of increasing by more than 100,000 couples annually, such households now make up some 50% of all households, with only 15% still having just a single breadwinner, in the old-fashioned way.

'Double-earners' are not always married. For some years now Dutch law has given couples (of mixed gender or the same sex) living together in a so-called 'registered partnership' virtually the same legal status as officially married couples. Since this law came into force many people have decided to 'live together' in a permanent, or at least long-lasting, relationship. To some people from non-western countries this comes as a shock: *'How about this living together, doesn't society find it a disgrace? What about fornication?'* (Tanzania)

Indeed, it *was* a social disgrace before the 1960s. In that decade living together started among urban intellectuals and artists, but it later spread to all levels of society. Nowadays even people affiliated to religious organisations have no problem living together outside marriage. The main reason is that people value mutual trust more than a legal bond, especially if they don't intend to have children. Nowadays, almost all couples who marry have already 'lived together' for a period of time. (In a way, this is another example of the Dutch not caring very much about authority, the state, the church!) This arrangement might be one factor explaining why, age-wise, Dutch women are 'world champions' in the field of having their first child: on average this only happens when they are 29 years old! *'In Japan it is far less accepted when someone in her thirties like me is not yet married and does not have children. The Netherlands is much freer in that respect.'*

Easy consumers   Since people living together are found mostly in the cities and are often higher educated than married couples, they earn higher average incomes. (For tax purposes they can choose to keep their incomes separate or to join them, depending on both partners' income and on their relationship.) They are usually hard working and have no children, and are therefore an attractive target group for people marketing time-saving devices and luxury products. Lured by flashy ads for loans with 'easy' repayments, they not only go in for a house or apart-ment with a high mortgage, but also for a second car, expensive furniture and kitchen equipment or a boat in a marina. The debts pile up, and although relatively they earn quite a lot of money, a growing number of such people run into financial trouble.

Sexism and emancipated men   This general picture is still an under-representation of women in the Dutch labour market and, as a matter of fact, also in politics and other important sectors. Over the years many Dutch women, with or without feminist sympathies, did not like their situation, discussed it, protested against it. Their pro-test has resulted in quite radical changes in recent decades. As in other countries, there have been campaigns for positive discrimina-tion of women, campaigns for encouraging girls to take university courses in traditionally male subjects such as technology and math-ematics. They have had some effect, women say, but changing the law is one thing, changing attitudes is another. It seems that the *polder model* – one of its effects being job-creation – has had more effect in bringing women into the labour market than any official campaign. The number of women in work has risen considerably in recent years.

Sexism exists in the Netherlands, too, but it is slowly waning as more and more women come into the labour market. Working women in Holland, including women from other countries, complain of men's subtle discrimination or open harassment. *'Only here in Holland I found out about women's problems. In Turkey I never felt second rank, there are more female architects, doctors and engineers in Turkey than in Holland. It is strange to suddenly realise that here women are treated as 'less clever'.'* (Turkey)

Legal and practical measures have been taken against open harassment, but the more subtle negative attitudes are more difficult to change. Especially in more technical branches the older generation of men still tends to 'joke' about women and overlook female talent. (Remember that 'political correctness' is less of an issue in Holland than in the USA). By not appreciating women's talents such men, and companies, lose a lot, according to this Argentinean (male) observer: *'The personality of Holland is female. Women here are more intelligent, more attractive, better looking, stronger, more powerful than men. I admire them very much. They are better managers, they will give you an honest answer, you can trust them.'* (Argentine)

Foreigners also observe that Dutch men seem to be quite emancipated: you see them shopping for food, carrying babies on their back, pushing prams, taking the kids for a walk. Especially among urban well-educated 'double earners', men do some of the household chores: quite a few regularly cook dinner, some do some of the cleaning jobs. *'It is surprising to see so many men doing the domestic tasks.'* (Philippines). Not everybody thinks they do enough: *'Men in Dutch society depend too much on the woman.'* (Denmark) This may still be true in more traditional families, but among young urban couples the division of household chores is coming closer and closer to 50%, albeit often with the help of hired cleaners and caterers. Socially, such couples leave each other quite free to pursue not only their careers but also their leisure time pursuits, accepting that they may have different interests and different friends: *'Here I have freedom. It is perfectly normal for a married woman to have friends of her own, to go dining somewhere without your husband. You can do what you like here. We don't have children, although we've been married for four years. In my country everybody wants to know why not. They think I'm crazy, everyone there has two children because that's the way it should be. Luckily here they don't.'* (Czech Republic)

Children and youngsters   Although it is not really a subject directly related to business, I would like to say something more about children and age in general, because so many visitors from Africa and Asia wonder: *'Where are the children?'* or *'How come I see so many old people?'* The birth rate in the Netherlands is low. It is known that birth rates generally decline as countries develop. Children are not needed to provide extra income or to care for their parents when they grow old, and child mortality rates decline rapidly. This means that just a few children 'will do'. This is a quite recent phenomenon, however. In past decades Holland's population increased very rapidly – from just 8 million around 1920 to 12 in the 1960s, to 16 today.

From the 1970s onward, however, the average Dutch family has had just two children. There is something of a baby boom going on at present, with some families having a third or even a fourth child, but so far this has had more influence on baby clinics than on national birth rates, since many other people don't have a family in the traditional sense, preferring to remain single or live together without having children. Moreover, a large share of the birth rate is taken up by children of ethnic groups in Holland, reflecting their more 'traditional' life styles. In some areas of cities such as Amsterdam and Rotterdam school classes consist mostly or even exclusively of 'ethnic' children.

As they reach secondary school age Dutch children begin to start negotiate more freedom from their parents: first the freedom to choose their own clothes, to go to school parties and come home late. A few years later they demand to be allowed to drink beer and to go to dances and discos, to go on holiday with their friends rather than with their parents. Gradually they stretch their independence. Money isn't generally a problem for Dutch children. Parents tend to be generous with pocket money, and many have part-time jobs or scholarships. (Although Holland may not be the best market for children's products, the young share in the general prosperity and spend freely on things such as fashion, music and entertainment). Many go to school camps at an early age, a few years later they may go on special youth holidays. As parental control decreases, not every-one can handle this independence: at weekends there are frequently problems with groups of drunken youngsters. But, they are the exception; the main interests of the majority of young people in the Netherlands are study and career.

Obviously, to compete successfully in the present day market-oriented and flexible job market, people need good education. So young people learn and learn. On average, they study up to the age of 18, but many study longer. Dutch youngsters are no longer very concerned about their future. Given the continuously favourable labour market, they feel that if they study and work hard enough, it will be easy to find a satisfactory job, a good position in society. The English term 'Go for it!' was recently given a literal Dutch translation. But they want more out of life than just a quiet job and a fixed salary. Surveys have revealed that Dutch youngsters find personal development, a good atmosphere and friendly relations with colleagues at least as important as money. *'Dutch youngsters love challenge. If I have a technical problem, they rush in to solve it. Everybody has good ideas. But they lose interest when a solution is found. In fact you should give them something new everyday, because they don't like routine.'* (Morocco)

Some people wonder what will happen to all their self-confidence if the economic tide turns....

Older people   With low birth rates and – in spite of its shortcomings – good health care, there are more older people in Dutch society than young. The baby boomers of the 1940s and 50s have reached the top of the labour market but here I want to focus on *their* parents and grandparents, the real old people.

The 'greying' or ageing of the Netherlands is under way, although at a somewhat slower pace than elsewhere in western Europe. A woman can now expect to live to about eighty, a man a little less. For present-day children the prospects are even better.

What does this mean as far as society in general and business in particular are concerned? It means a general restructuring will be necessary. More older people means that there is an increasing demand for specialised health care and more money is needed to provide pensions. As the working population decreases, tax revenues decrease, and in the future this may present problems in financing the needs of large non-working groups of people. In 2000, newspapers reports said that over the next fifty years European countries will need many *millions* of immigrants in order to pay for old-age pensions, to replace retired workers, even to keep the population stable or growing. The Netherlands is small and cramped already and with growing concerns about the multicultural society other solutions may be more appropriate. Government and financial institutions are urging people to make private provisions for their old age rather than depend on state pensions.

Real problems are foreseen for the years after 2010, when the 'post war baby boomers' will reach retirement age. But then, what *is* 'the retirement age'? Officially it is 65, but: *'I have the impression that virtually nobody here works until the age of sixty-five.'* (USA).

This observation is correct to some extent. Many people take early retirement, because they have private savings, special arrangements with their insurance company, or prefer to take the 'freedom-with-less-money' option. The pensionable age of government workers has been made flexible, and in companies, too, arrangements can be made, although at considerable cost to the person involved. There is also another, quite contradictory, trend: with the 'greying' of Holland and the lack of skilled workers, employers are calling for people to work *over* the age of 65, rather than retire early, and offer bonuses to people willing to do so. But in a March 2000 survey most people said they would prefer to retire at 59!

Old age provisions Given the long life expectancy of the Dutch, once they retire they can still expect to enjoy a pleasant life for many years. As in many western countries there are good provisions for the elderly, but foreigners do not always understand: *'I was extremely shocked to find that this (Dutch) family I visited had sent their own mother to a home for the aged, while having a dog sit on the sofa as if it were a family member.'* (Tanzania). At first most Dutch people will react with smiling surprise but, thinking about it, will agree that it must look strange. But there is a story behind it.

The average Dutch family is nuclear: Dad, Mum and the kids. The kids have a lot of freedom, their own room, their own music, usually their own TV set and their own computer. But Dutch houses are not large and grandparents don't want to bother their (hard working) children, and don't want to be bothered by loud music. They often prefer to stay in their own home as long as possible. This independence is encouraged by the government and there are organisations providing meals, cleaning services and basic medical care. Many old people may prefer this themselves and it should be said that there is a long tradition in Holland of older people living apart from their children, even if it is only in a separate part of the family farm or in a separate room. As early as the 17th century there were homes for the elderly, either run by churches or by municipal authorities.

Nowadays, if circumstances no longer allow them to live in their own house, old people can move into one of the quiet, comfortable homes where they can live independently but with some degree of household and medical assistance. If their health deteriorates too much there are special homes for the disabled elderly which provide full care, including recreational and medical facilities. To people from countries where family members support each other through thick and thin (even if the main reason is a lack of social benefits) this organised old-age care ('mechanical solidarity') is perceived as cold and impersonal. It is very hard to explain to them how it all feels from the Dutch perspective. African people especially give me very negative comments, but this one comes from a Pakistani businessman who visits Holland regularly: *'I was shocked by the treatment of aged people, by the living together of non-married people, by the loose sexual morals.'*

Indeed there are cases when the situation is very sad, for example for old people without children who totally depend on outside assistance from government or charitable organisations. Unfortunately the following observation is correct: *'There are many people here who feel alone. You read more and more about elderly people found dead in their home. When recently I heard about a woman who gets money just to visit an old lady, I was happy to be Turkish. With us that is different.'*

Personal independence and social cohesion   *'People are nice here, but they don't make an effort to get into touch with you. They leave you alone too much. In the apartment where I live, they helped me when I locked myself out, but afterwards they were at a distance again.'* (South Africa)

Yes, Dutch society, like other western cultures, is 'atomising': individualism is increasing and it shocks people from more 'collectivist' cultures: *'I think Dutch people don't want to get involved with each other.'* (Iran)

Mental problems   One observer takes it even further: *'It strikes me that there are so many people here with mental problems. Everybody has money here, but many people are alone at home, with nothing to do. They start worrying and go mad.'* (Papua New Guinea). Of course, like in any country, there are people in Dutch society with mental problems and illnesses, but there is an extensive psychiatric network to monitor and help them. If the patients' behaviour is reasonably 'normal' neighbours will usually keep in touch with them. But an increasing number of people neglect themselves to such an extent that they lose their home and join the homeless who can be seen roaming about the large cities. Because they do not have an official formal address, they are not entitled to social benefits. Church volunteers and professional organisations provide them with some basic facilities and try to get them back on their feet. But it should be added that, as in all

areas of health care, the psychiatric branch suffers from a
shortage of professionals and volunteers, and sometimes from
too drastic economising. The latter problem will now be solved,
the government has promised, but the first one remains...

Most people quite like their independence and become uneasy when
they feel it is threatened. Many people live alone – nation-wide, single,
divorced or widowed people represent some 35% of all households. In
the larger cities sometimes more than 50% of households are single-
person households. Now living alone is not always the same thing as
loneliness, but people from other countries often find this difficult to
accept. *'Not everyone is like that (stand-offish), but most people are. The
way of life here is very sad to me. I can't get used to it, no matter how long
I live here. All this strong individualism. Everyone for himself.'* (Cameroon)

Just like their married or cohabiting counterparts single people
have their friends and colleagues, their hobbies and sports clubs,
their theatre visits, etc. This implies that even single people's leisure
time is often highly structured, not by the family, but by the 8 o'clock
start of the above activities.

The separation of work and leisure time is important to the Dutch.
Small wonder this observation was made: *'It is very hard to get your
Dutch colleagues to go for a beer after work, at least I haven't succeeded in
that yet.'* (Finland). In the current, more flexible economy, many
people try to negotiate flexible work hours in order to arrive at an
optimal balance with their private life, for example, sharing childcare
with their partner who also works. Given the tight labour market,
quite a few employers accede to such requests. Some experimentation with 'tele-working' has started in branches such as insurance,
where people can partly work from home.

An increase in one-person households obviously has consequences
for 'the market' – each household needs essentials such as a
refrigerator, a television, and so on, and more and more small one-
person portions of food and other products are being sold. When
marketing or selling in Holland, business people from other countries
might like to keep this in mind.

Individualists or collectivists?   The Dutch see themselves as individualists, and looked at in a global context, they
are. When observing them in public life one gets that impression,
too. This makes outsiders think that their entire lives are like

that. But in private life and in the work place, too, the Dutch definitely have a collectivist aspect, as symbolised by the term *gezellig*. They like regular get-togethers with their family and friends, having coffee together or attending a birthday party. Many are members of clubs or other organisations and have long-term subscriptions to ideologically or religiously based news-papers or TV-magazines. Streets, neigbourhoods, even villages, may have festive committees and community centres, although this is generally among people with lower-level incomes. At work people appreciate a certain togetherness with departmental colleagues, which may easily extend to the canteen.

One last aspect of individualism affecting visitors from other countries should be mentioned therefore. Dutch people being quite individual-istic, they assume that everyone is like that and prefers to be left alone, free to make their own choices – in fact, the literal translation of the Dutch word for hospitality, *gastvrijheid*, is guest-freedom! So colleagues, trainees and business colleagues from abroad are not always given the kind of hospitality that they themselves might extend to guests at home.

In Holland, invitations are given for set evenings or weekends. Then the Dutch hosts will prepair a good meal, set the table nicely, select music to please their guest, take them out somewhere they feel will interest them, etc. In short: they do their best to make things *'gezellig'*. The guests get all the family's attention and anyone dropp-ing in or phoning will be put off – remember the Dutch are 'mono-chronic'. But this shower of attention lasts only as long as that particular dinner party, that particular one-day excursion. Western visitors have little problem with this aspect of the Dutch character: *'I always found Dutchmen very hospitable. All right, you must make an arrangement to visit them and I had to get used to that. But once the arrangement is made, they receive you very well.'* (Iceland) And: *'Our neighbours are friendly, they have invited us twice for tea and they give us good advice on how to do things, for example in finding a hospital for childbirth.'* (Japan)

But a lady from India commented: *'In India we had Dutch expatriates for neighbours. We went to their house to say hello, welcomed them with a dinner party and offered our help. When we moved to Holland, we expected the same in reverse, but nobody came. I had to go and ask them in. Only then they came. That was very disappointing to us, but I must add that later they were very nice to us.'* I can imagine the initial disappointment, but readers should be reminded that privacy is a major concept in Holland. Dutch neighbours are afraid of intruding upon people who are still settling in, perhaps cleaning and redecorating their new house or apartment, arranging their furniture, setting up their household. Remember the section on charity: the Dutch are sensitive to anyone who needs help, but they also respect people's privacy. Help is almost always given – but only if asked for.

So the Dutch think themselves to be very hospitable, always doing their best to please their guests. But given their sense of privacy, their many private activities and their family-orientation, Dutch hospitality does not imply a non-stop welcome at any given time – access is restricted. To people from countries where the door is always open for anyone to drop in, this is disappointing:

1. All figures mentioned in this chapter were found in articles in *NRC-Handelsblad* newspaper.

2. 86% of women under 30, with or without a partner but without children, work.

3. Unlike in other languages, in Dutch there is a single word – *'gezin'* – which distinguishes the nuclear family from the extended family, for which the word *'familie'* is used.

Chapter 11

ON ETHNIC VARIETY

'Those who have Dutch blood in their veins, free of foreign taint'
(first line of Dutch national anthem in the 19th century,
long since abolished)

Visiting business people and expatriates living in the Netherlands cannot fail to notice that they are not the only people of foreign descent. In this chapter I shall focus on people of non-Dutch origin who are permanently residing in the Netherlands. Nonetheless when they get in touch with the 'alien police' for registration and residence permits, temporary expatriates will encounter more or less the same aspects of Dutch immigration policy as people seeking permanent residence. There is a whole story behind Dutch immigration policy.

'Allochtonen'   The presence in the Netherlands of ethnic minorities and other groups from foreign countries is quite controversial. It is estimated that some 10 to 15% of the present population of 16 million were not born here, or at least one of their parents was not.[1] This is the criterion officially in use for defining *allochtonen*, a word of Greek origin meaning 'born elsewhere', used to indicate this widely varied group. *'I was shocked to find they have a special word for everyone not born here.'* (South Africa) About half of them are people from former colonies who already had Dutch citizenship when they arrived. Exact numbers on *allochtonen* are not known because of a legal prohibition on registering race or descent and the differing degrees of residence in the country.

There may be prosperity in the country as a whole, but among the *allochtonen* unemployment is three to four times higher than among the native Dutch, and salaries are on average 22% lower. The lower average income can be largely explained by lower levels of education, a lower average age (of workers) and a higher share of part-time work, but, of course, on the issue of the unemployment figures discrimination must also play some role. The some 14 million opinions of the native Dutch on all the aspects of the changing social climate produce a confusing mix of lively debate, moving expressions of goodwill, social tensions and sometimes outright racist ideas. *'Generally speaking, people here treat us elegantly. But some of them do make you feel you are from a poor country.'* (Bangladesh)

Different cultural characteristics   The Netherlands never really perceived itself as a country of immigration until the 1970s. Some immigration of Iberian *Jews* and French *Huguenots* occurred long ago, immediately after the Dutch republic allowed people religious freedom. Later, in the 1930s, a group of *Chinese* found shelter in Holland when the Dutch shipping companies they had worked for went bankrupt in the severe economic crisis. But these arrivals were felt to have been unique historical events and, anyway, they only involved comparatively small groups.

In fact, there was quite a lot of migration *from* Holland after the Second World War. In the bleak post-war years, when the Cold War cast an uncomfortable shadow across the whole of Europe, some 300.000 Dutch people left to start new lives in countries such as Australia, New Zealand, the USA and Canada. Even nowadays some Dutch people are still leaving. In recent years the tight restrictions imposed by the European Union, falling prices for their products and the astronomical cost of land has persuaded (or forced) large numbers of farmers to move into new markets in Canada, Denmark and – somewhat surprisingly – eastern Europe. But this goes against the trend: many more people arrive in this country than leave it, but it was only in 1998 that the government officially recognised this fact and created a new 'Ministry of Large Cities Policy and Integration'.

The effect of this belated acknowledgement of what had long been reality was, and to some extent still is, that unlike the true immigration countries mentioned above, the Netherlands had never developed official procedures for mass immigration. No introduction programmes had been set up, no obligatory language classes, no nation-wide policies for providing housing, education and jobs to newcomers. There seemed to be no need for this when mass immigration started around 1950, since the first group (former colonials from Indonesia) already spoke Dutch and were reasonably familiar with Dutch culture and the Dutch way of life. In 1975, more former colonials arrived, this time from Suriname, and they were soon followed by people from the Netherlands Antilles, again nearly all of them speaking Dutch. Their integration was reasonably successful.

During the 1960s, the Dutch economy was booming and the nation could afford to offer its young people a good and extended education. This resulted in a serious shortage of blue collar workers and, as in surrounding countries, work contracts were given to unskilled labourers from rural communities in less prosperous nations around the Mediterranean: particularly *Morocco* and *Turkey*.

The 'guest workers', as they were called, had hoped to earn quick money and send it home to their relatives. But life in Holland was far more expensive than they had foreseen. If they were lucky, their work contract was prolonged, and they stayed. Most of the other nationalities returned home, but the Moroccans and Turks stayed on. The Dutch government permitted their wives and children to join them, and for the first time these families left their rural surroundings and came to live in foreign, urbanised Holland. They often found housing in dilapidated, cheap blocks built during the industrial revolution of the 1880s. If they could afford it Dutch working class people were moving away from such areas to greener suburbs. Through the same mechanism, the older suburbs from the 1950s and 60s also became increasingly 'ethnic'. In these decaying neighbourhoods, the immigrants opened shops to cater for their needs, and organised places of worship and community centres. Gradually all the larger cities of Holland saw the rise of ethnic groups with a totally different culture, living mostly in working class areas outside the city centres. There are now an estimated 300,000 people of Turkish origin or descent and 250,000 of Moroccan living in the Netherlands. Most of the 'first generation' have retained their original nationality, since dual nationality is either legally impossible or considered undesirable in their country of origin.

Up to the 1980s the Dutch economy generally thrived, and there was little competition for jobs from the 'foreign' workers. But then things changed: unemployment rose among the Dutch, but it rose much more among the immigrant workers. Although they had paid their taxes and social premiums for years, there was growing resentment to the fact that they were just as entitled to the protection of the extensive Dutch social benefits system as anyone else.

At a time when on international television fierce-looking groups of extremists were violently advocating Islamic revolution, in the Netherlands irritation about the foreigners' cultural habits, their women's scarves, their Muslim beliefs, were voiced more and more openly. Authorities and individuals alike began to worry about potential ethnic violence.

Individual towns took their own measures, applied their own procedures, while all kinds of organisations, official and private, also developed their own activities. Although such initiatives were financially assisted by the government, there still was no overall policy, and this resulted in a confusing patchwork of small-scale solutions. Only in the 1980s, when permanent ethnic minorities started forming from these groups (at a time when the economic climate was unfavourable and there was high unemployment) did the need for a more overall policy become urgent. At the same time the influx of asylum seekers from countries all over the world also demanded action. But it appears to have been a case of too little too late, and the introductory citizenship and language programmes are not proving to be very successful. There is not enough people to execute them, there are waiting lists, and there is far too much bureaucratic red tape. Moreover, suddenly making such programmes obligatory is difficult to accept for target groups, which have been ignored, or at least neglected, for years.

Asylum seekers   Ever since the 1970s Europe has witnessed an increase in the number of legal and illegal *refugees,* arriving from countries all over the world, requesting political asylum. Civil war, political repression, religious persecution and economic misery cause people to look for a better life in wealthy and peaceful countries like the Netherlands. Authorities try to distinguish between real *political refugees* and fortune seekers ('economic refugees'). They are under pressure from sections of the public fearing abuse of the social benefit system which will then have to be financed by increased taxes, the loss of the established peaceful social order, religious fanaticism or even, in the case of the Netherlands, still greater over-population. In 1999, the largest groups of *asylum seekers* arriving to the Netherlands came from Afghanistan (over 4000), Iraq (3900), former Yugoslavia (3850), Somalia, Azerbaijan, Sudan, Angola, Iran, Turkey and Sierra Leone.

Both in absolute and relative figures, the Netherlands receive the second highest number of asylum seekers in Europe (after Germany), and the government institution set up to check the validity of all these people's stories, decide which are genuine and then channel the ones admitted into Dutch society, is grossly overburdened. One effect is that people not yet legally admitted have to wait endlessly in special centres, where they are not allowed to work. They are not even allowed to learn Dutch, since that might indicate they can stay.

Tragic stories of depression and loss of self-respect are received by the Dutch media, but at the same time there is increasing pressure on the authorities crack down on what are seen as 'bogus' asylum seekers. With stricter criteria, Holland hopes to deter people from coming here, but the country's prosperity and its good human rights reputation mean that more and more continue to arrive. Because of the shortage of labour, there is currently some discussion about whether to allow asylum seekers to join the Dutch labour market – at least temporarily. Those finally admitted are supported by job mediation and integration programmes.

Yet some people fall victim to the growing Dutch suspicion of 'foreigners': *'I got so angry when this police officer told me: 'This cannot be your car!' Just because I look a bit different and speak Dutch with an accent!'* (Serbia) And: *'When I applied for a visa at the Dutch embassy in Moscow, they treated my really badly.'* (Russian management trainee) After the opening up of eastern Europe, Holland faced an increase of immigration from those relatively nearby countries. Unfortunately not all of them come here to work and contribute to society. In Holland, too, the good suffer from the criminal behaviour of the bad.

Multicultural society   The effects of immigration in Dutch society are manifold and complex. In line with liberal, tolerant Dutch society, everyone is free to live in the way they want. The Dutch education system allows non-Dutch children to learn their parents' language and religion, many ethnic organisations are subsidised, freedom of expression and political views applies to *allochtonen* as to any other citizen, and so forth. A young waitress of Turkish descent said: *'The thing I like most about the Netherlands is the level of tolerance. Regardless of whether you're black or white, man or woman, hooker or stewardess – no one gets in your way.'*

In spite of the Serbian's bad experience, I think the quote given in the previous edition still holds: *'Generally speaking, there is an atmosphere here of tolerance, equality and equal rights. In other so-called developed countries the locals act as if they're superior and they behave dominantly. Of course here too there are some people who act strangely and discriminate in subtle ways, but the majority is tolerant and hospitable to foreigners.'* (Cambodia) And a Japanese adds: *'Children here don't sit up at all if a new kid in class looks quite different, but we didn't know that before we came. My kids expected to be in a school full of pink children with white hair.'*

Now all of this may sound rather wonderful, but not all is sweetness and light, either among the native Dutch or among the immigrants' groups themselves. The so-called multi-cultural society is not developing without heated debate. Dutch society as a whole may appear to be tolerant, but as we saw before, not every individual in it is. There has been underground grumbling about some ethnic groups and their lifestyles for decades, but until the 1990s this was considered 'politically incorrect', certainly among the better educated. It was a bit of a dogma that in a society of minorities, all groups had the right to lead their own life, particularly those in weaker positions, such as the ethnic groups. Words like 'discrimination' and 'racism' were frequently heard and all parties except those on the extreme right wing tried to avoid any suggestion of this.

But then a politician from a respectable party broke the taboo, openly bringing the issue into open debate. This stimulated other individuals and parties to share their – until then covert – views in more detail. From then on statistics on problems, low education and rising crime among ethnic people were published more openly, inviting new debate. In 1999, a newspaper article named 'The multicultural drama'[2] triggered a media discussion on the desirability of mutual cultural adaptation, the faults (of course…) and limitations of the Dutch policy on the issue so far, and the lessons to be learned from all this. Again questions arose concerning the freedom Dutch society should give to people following norms and values contrary to the ones current in Holland. Aren't we a bit too liberal? Shouldn't Dutch cultural values be defended more strongly? But in a pluriform land of subcultures, with somewhat hazy concepts of tolerance and privacy, what exactly *are* 'Dutch values'? How far can demands of integration stretch? What are the criteria?

As this discussion went on several things occurred that made it all the more urgent. It was discovered that some asylum seekers had had their young daughters circumcised; Holland's first 'highschool shooting' turned out to be a case of Islamic 'revenging family honour'; and the Dutch public was shocked to hear of outright conservative, anti-western sermons of some 'imported' religious leaders.

A Dutch police chief commissioner, probably also thinking of personnel shortage and the need for 'ethnic' officers on his force, suggested that, if need be, Muslim women should be allowed to wear headscarves while on police duty. This prompted jokes on the difficulties of designing a cap/scarf combination. But it was also pointed out that since female police officers in Turkey and Morocco do not wear headscarves, it would be taking tolerance too far.

But all in all, such issues are the exception: *'Nobody at university minds me wearing a headscarf. Quite the contrary: my fellow students admire me for it. (…) People in Turkey could hardly imagine the combination of a female student and a headscarf. That alone proves that the Netherlands is where I want to be. I'm too attached to my freedom. That doesn't mean I don't value Turkish culture, of course'* (Turkish student)

All the stories and statistics published in the press, all this debate, leads parts of the general Dutch public – perhaps less educated, perhaps living in areas where the ethnic mix is strongest – to feel rather overwhelmed by the changes that a multicultural society has brought. Conservative – and proud – as they may be about the accomplishments of Dutch society, they feel threatened by what seems to be an unstoppable flood of people who all want to come and live here. Quite a few fear that these immigrants will not truly blend in, sticking to their own culture and religion. Some complain quite loudly, others grumble in the privacy of their own homes, and there is also a great deal of silent opposition.

Racist?   In my personal opinion the vast majority of Dutch people are not really racists. This is proved by the fact that there are friendships, many racially mixed marriages (and 'living together'-s of course), and most people accept them. People of different racial backgrounds also co-operate quite well at various levels of society. In a comparative survey of European racism the Dutch were found to be no more (or less…) racist than citizens in surrounding countries. But what *does* matter to the Dutch, and what *does* make them discriminate, are signs of religious intolerance of the kind they themselves managed to overcome after centuries of fierce religious debate and strife.

In the debate on 'the multicultural drama', pleas were held to keep open the lines of communication, to remain on speaking terms, to prevent the kind of self-selected socio-religious *apartheid*[3] that ruled much of Dutch society until not so long ago. The Dutch government is trying to decrease concentrations of certain ethnic groups in particular areas. Spatial separation ('ghetto-formation' as it is called) must be avoided. But like the Dutch majority itself, most people from the ethnic groups prefer to live their lives within their own group, not mixing much with people from other groups. Among Dutch and non-Dutch citizens alike this leads to a continuation of stereotypes and prejudices about each other's cultures. *'It shocks me to hear the Dutch openly say negative things about whole categories of ethnic people. In the UK, racism happens on a more personal, individual level, here it seems to be generic.'* (Britain)

Ethnic dividing lines can easily evoke attitudes of 'us' and 'them', in spite of campaigns on television and street posters designed to overcome such feelings. At a personal level, more contact and communication are probably the best way to overcome prejudice and discrimination. This may be difficult to bring about, given the Dutch tendency to restrict one's private life to one's own group, but people should none-theless try – integration is a two-way process.

Fortunately, the Netherlands has a long tradition of living with 'people who think differently'[4], and in the process has developed social mechanisms to keep a balance between togetherness and separate-ness. Authorities do their best to solve or prevent conflicts, or to be humane to both sides. But things are not always well-balanced: *'Dutch-men pretend to be the conscience of the world. But you only need look about you or read the newspapers and you see a whole lot of discrimination. Here too, people are not treated equally.* (South Africa) *'People from Turkey or Morocco can only marginally participate, not in leading positions or in politics. Within Dutch organisations, foreigners get very few chances. People still think: if they can't speak Dutch exactly like us, their knowledge will probably be less also.'* (Turkish business woman)

Although Dutch society is still far from ideal, not much ethnic violence has occurred in the Netherlands so far. The Dutch solution to problems has always been: talk it over. Hopefully it will remain that way.

Finally   Dutch society, like most others, has become much more complex in recent years. There is a greater potential for social circum-stances to deteriorate into lawlessness. With increasing individualism and pluralism, disintegration of the social fabric can turn tolerance towards other groups into indifference and intolerance.

In the previous edition, besides 'an outcast position' I mentioned 'persistent unemployment' as a possible breeding ground for social unrest. At present, such unemployment has virtually disappeared, albeit not at quite the same rate in all ethnic groups. But a better socio-economic position doesn't solve everything, alas. In recent years, it has become obvious that in spite of all the prosperity quite a lot of people in Holland suffer from a deep dissatisfaction with life. Youngsters of *all* ethnic groups, including the Dutch, may be tempted into lawless and antisocial acts ranging from vandalism to drug deal-ing and violent crime, causing annoyance, fear and outrage among victims and the general public. Reports and rumours of hooliganism, violence, theft, drug abuse, and so on do nothing to appease the general feeling that society may be heading for hard times.

Only time will tell the final outcome – if such a thing as 'the final outcome' exists. Second and third generation immigrants blend in much more successfully than their parents. Speaking Dutch fluently, they reach higher education levels and find better jobs, thus coming into closer contact with their Dutch peers. Mixed marriages occur increasingly often, people meet in their place of work, in schools and shops, at sports clubs and other organisations. 'Positive discrimination', advocated (and sometimes practised) for some time, will hopefully soon be unnecessary, as second and third immigrants are increasingly able to participate in society on equal terms.

All such measures cost money and only general prosperity ensures social peace. Unless economic disaster occurs, there is a fair chance that in a few decades people with Turkish or Moroccan family names will be just as unnoticed in Dutch society as French or German names are now, that Asian or African features will become as 'socially invisible' as Indonesian ones are now.

Having explored the issue of cultural variety over the last decades, let's now turn to some regional varieties in Dutch culture.

1. Excluded from this figure are people from other European Union member states, who number some 300.000.
2. In *NRC-Handelsblad*, in an article by Paul Scheffer.
3. Probably the Dutch word best known internationally, through the South African variety of Dutch called Afrikaans. It literally means 'separateness'.
4. This term is one word in Dutch, *andersdenkenden*, an old expression used for people of another religion.

Chapter 12

REGIONS AND RANDSTAD

Netherlanders and Hollanders:
Regional diversity in a small country

There is more to the Netherlands than just 'Holland'. There is a distinct flavour of regionalism in many parts of the country – however small it may be. Let's make a tour of the country from north to south, before returning to the west.

Generally speaking, *northerners* and *easterners* are felt to be less outspoken and more sociable than people from the dominant Randstad area. They have a reputation of being more introverted, not using a lot of words if something can be said with just a few. This may reflect their less – until recently – largely agricultural orientation, with intensive exposure to the speedy pace of modern-day business life and to foreign contacts.

Regionalism is quite strong in the northern province of *Friesland*. Among themselves Frisians speak their own language (Fries, or as they say Frysk, a separate branch of the Germanic language family, akin to Dutch, English and Danish). They are the descendants of tribes described by the Romans as fierce warriors. They are said to be hardworking and, once you have gained their trust, very loyal, but watch out: they also have a touch of anti-authoritarianism and, if provoked, easily lose their temper! There is a drive for cultural autonomy: local media are popular and in 1996 the name of the province was officially changed to *Fryslân*. Towns have names in both Frisian and Dutch, and primary education is partly in the local language. To the Dutch the province evokes an image of milk and cows, lakes, ice-skating, dark-sailed ships and villages on man-made hillocks (*terpen*).

Culturally, *Groningen* enjoys a less distinctive image than Friesland, but economically it is important because of the enormous quantities of natural gas, providing high quality gas for the Netherlands and large parts of western Europe. Yet Groningen as a province rather lags behind the rest of the country, with a lower average income and more unemployment than elsewhere. Inviting new investments, it promotes its spaciousness and quality of life with a hint of its northernmost position on the map: 'There is nothing above Groningen!'

The image of the provinces of *Drenthe*, *Overijssel* and *Gelderland* is mostly based on their wooded and hilly areas. They are popular for holidays and among retired people from the Randstad looking for somewhere else to live. Life is more relaxed than in the west, and there are many charming old towns. In the mid-1990s, the Gelderland river area called the Betuwe received international press attention when it was threatened by potentially disastrous flooding. Dyke improvements, 'the River Delta Plan', have since been made.

The Bible Belt Not a province in itself, this narrow band of land stretching diagonally through the country (from northwestern Overijssel down to the islands of Zeeland) has a very particular variety of Dutch culture. This 'Dutch Bible Belt' is a largely rural area with a high proportion of orthodox Calvinists. Here social life is still strongly dictated by fundamentalist interpretations of the Bible: frequent church attendance and absolute observance of Sunday as a day without work. Both insurance and vaccinations may be considered as opposing God's will, and they abhor the modern aspects of city life, including television. On the basis of different interpretations of the Bible (hard to follow for outsiders), this group is subdivided into various denominations, political parties and related institutions such as schools, etc. Referring to their stern dress sense, other Dutchmen call them 'black stocking churches'. It was from these circles that, in 2000, a draft amendment giving workers the right to refuse to work on Sundays was presented to the Dutch parliament. Employers and their favourite party, the VVD, voted against this amendment, but all other political parties – albeit for various other reasons of their own – supported it.

Before turning to the south, something should be said about a province almost without any image at all: the newest province, *Flevoland* officially inaugurated in 1985. For centuries the area was part of the Zuiderzee, a large body of seawater in the heart of the country, and it contained two tiny islands. After devastating floods in 1916 it was decided that it should be enclosed and partially reclaimed. Flevoland is the result of decades of hard work by thousands of people, a 'high-tech' province of straight lines. *'This is incredible! Isn't it amazing to realise that all of this is not just nature but man-made land!'* (USA)

Obviously, it takes time for cultural identity and natural beauty to develop but below all this modernity there *is* a past after all. Long ago, before disappearing under the waters of the Zuiderzee, much of this area was dry land and recent excavations have brought to light graves dating from about 5000BC. Such things might make you think twice about a question I was asked – with some hesitance – on a special KIT-programme for young African healthcare workers: *'With all this taking land from the sea, aren't you Dutch afraid of nature taking revenge…?'*

Now let us turn to the south. In contrast to the rest of the nation, *southerners* are felt to be more outgoing, enjoying life's pleasures more, taking more time for their personal life. They are also slightly less individualistic, and more oriented towards relatives and people from their home town. This may result in outsiders – whether Dutch or from other countries – having a hard time being accepted into local communities. Finally, southerners are also felt to be less egalitarian, more hierarchic, more respectful to authorities such as their boss, the church authorities and political figures. Both outsiders and the southerners themselves point out that all this is related to the fact that 'the South' – the part of the country which lies south of 'the big rivers' (Rhine, Waal and Maas), except for the province of Zeeland – was never Calvinistic. After the 1500s it remained Catholic when the rest of the country became Protestant. Hofstede suggests that this Catholic part of the Netherlands might, culturally speaking, be classified as the northernmost part of Latin Europe, while the rest of the country could be called the southernmost part of Scandinavia. Some of these perceptions may be stereotypical, but they do contain a grain of truth.

The large province called *Noord-Brabant* is now highly urbanised and the most industrialised province in the country. But to the Dutch it still evokes images of a slightly Latin ambiance that includes carnival celebrations in February, and large and sociable families enjoying food and drinks together. The image reflects the past, a feudal society of rich and noble families owning sandy and infertile land worked by poor peasants. As late as 1885, Van Gogh painted the 'Potato Eaters' and other images of grinding poverty. Something of this still lingers in some villages, but 'immigration' from other provinces has virtually erased this aspect of life.

Together with Limburg, Brabant remained Catholic during and after the Reformation. Possibly as a result of the stricter feudal and Catholic hierarchy, people from Brabant also have the reputation of being more respectful to authorities, less openly critical, less blunt. In the business-world this may lead to more attention to 'representation': lunches and dinners, dressing up for business occasions, slightly more formal manners, taking more time to get to know each other better. Just a touch of the Latin mentality.

This feeling is even stronger with people from the province of *Limburg*. The extreme geographical position and the strange shape of this province suggest that it might easily have become part of Belgium or Germany had history taken a slightly different turn. Indeed, its character is in no way 'typically Dutch' especially in the south. There we find rolling hills, another type of farm and village, a distinctly different lifestyle and a strong dialect, barely understandable to northern listeners. Its most distinctive feature is the so-called 'soft G' (also heard in Noord-Brabant), a rather more charming way of pronouncing this letter than the 'hard' G in official Dutch.

Limburg's capital city of Maastricht can be called the most Latin city of the Netherlands: *'Sometimes I go to Maastricht. It is more formal there than in Amsterdam, but I like being there. People are happier, more open, they are not Calvinistic. I feel related to them. Calvinists are even more religious and stern than the Irish.'* (Ireland)

Limburg hints at all this un-Dutchness in tourist advertisements up north: 'Come visit our own foreign country'. For other purposes it advertises its 'Euregion' character, with German and Belgian industries nearby, in a bid to attract foreign business people and other visitors.

Limburg's business culture is more like that in southern Europe: less down-to-earth behaviour, a little more ceremony, more time for initial contact, less outspoken criticism, more chance of being invited out to lunch or dinner. But a number of 'incidents' exhaustively reported in the regional and national press also proved less conventional business practices.

Finally, we turn to *Zeeland*, the only southern province which is mostly Protestant, and therefore, culturally speaking, belonging to the north rather than the south, although it has a distinct flavour of its own. The province has many water-related connections: islands, waterways, beaches, oysters and mussels. Until the 1960s this island-province was not only isolated from the rest of the country it was also isolated internally – which explains the differences between islands and villages, as well as the low population density.

Zeeland has suffered from regular flooding. Only after the devastating floods of 1953, in which more than 1800 people died, the rest of the country realised that something should be done. The Delta Plan was soon underway. This plan envisaged a complex of huge and ingenious dams keeping out the sea from between the islands and connecting the islands to the mainland. It changed the character of the communities in the province, even before the final dam was closed in 1985, as Dutch and later German tourists discovered the beauty of the islands, and as people from Zeeland began to commute to work in Europoort and Rotterdam harbour, reinforcing the 'northern' mentality.

Randstad   So all of this is *not* the Randstad. Then, people from overseas might still wonder, what *is* the Randstad? The introductory chapter mentioned how the Randstad is the dominant area of the country. Here I will add something about its geographical, economic and cultural structure.

The word Randstad[2], meaning 'ring-city' or 'edge-city', was coined not that long ago for the cluster of cities in the west which encircle a rather unpopulated agricultural area in the provinces of Noord-Holland, Zuid-Holland and Utrecht. It includes small cities as Dordrecht, Delft, Leiden, Haarlem, Zaanstad and Hilversum and four main centres: Rotterdam (agglomeration: 1.1 million inhabitants), The Hague (700,000), Amsterdam (1.1 million) and Utrecht (550,000). Taken together, these cities and the adjoining towns and villages form a metropolis of more than six million people. The economic and cultural activities taking place in the Randstad make living there attractive to many and further growth is expected (and feared). When they travel through the region, people from other countries may see it as one large conglomeration, but only in recent years, with increasing mobility, has a kind of shared urban identity grown up. Individual cities and villages still boast their own dialect, mentality, history, traditions and culture.

Rotterdam: the busy economic heart of the country is the most modern Dutch city, being continuously rebuilt since the 1940 Nazi bombing raids destroyed the old city centre. Rotterdam is home to many important economic and scientific activities. Its port areas stretch for over 30 km to the sea and are home to shipping and shipping-related companies, huge oil refineries, and Europe's largest cargo storage areas. In fact, Rotterdam is the main harbour for the German Ruhr region, with which it is connected by excellent inland waterways, the Rhine and Waal rivers. In terms of mentality, its inhabitants are known to be very pragmatic, hardworking, money-minded and somewhat chauvinistic.

The Hague (Den Haag in Dutch): the country's political centre (but *not* the official capital). The city is home to the Dutch Parliament and its ministries, to the foreign embassies and the International Court of Justice. Royal Dutch Shell's headquarters are also here, as well as numerous national organisations. In spite of the many activities which take place there, it has remained a quiet, green city, where many foreign expatriates choose to live. Other Dutch people do not always appreciate the Hagueners' slightly formal life styles, accusing them of 'window dressing'. The city also has some less well-to-do areas east of the centre.

Schiphol, the international airport of Amsterdam wants to be the 'Gateway to Europe'. Once a lake, it is almost a city now, home to hundreds of companies which provide the myriad of services Europe's fourth busiest airport demands.

Amsterdam: the official capital and home to Holland's cultural elite and to thousands of non-conformists (see chapter 8). Amsterdammers are fiercely chauvinistic about their city's avant-garde position and its somewhat mixed reputation. They are the most extrovert of all the northerners, partly due to influxes of people from Brabant and Flanders long ago. The city's proverbial humour and its dialect still reflect the city's former Jewish subculture.

But Amsterdam's reputation often makes people forget that the city is also a booming business centre. It is home to the Dutch stock exchange, to the headquarters of a number of Dutch and international banks, ICT, the diamond industry and a number of graphic industries, including national newspapers.

Utrecht: the hub of the Dutch railway network (including its headquarters), boasts the country's largest exhibition and fair grounds and its biggest shopping mall. Utrecht is also the traditional capital of the Dutch Catholic church, as well as a number of other denominations. Its student population (the country's largest university is located here) has changed the outdated reputation of Utrechters being somewhat introverted and 'stiff'.

The Green Heart   The areas between these cities, the so-called *Green Heart*, and the surrounding areas of the two Holland provinces are still relatively scarcely populated and, until recently, largely agricultural: green pastures with cows, straight draining ditches and meandering rivers, old farms and quaint villages, and towns. But the region is coming under heavy pressure from the surrounding cities and their surplus population.

Within the Green Heart, Schiphol Airport is eating away at rural land, while new motorways and railway connections (including a projected high-speed link to Paris) threaten to disturb the rural calm, and the huge volume of traffic creates jams all around the cities. The inhabitants and environmentalists worry about all these developments and protest against them.

So far, people visiting or coming to live in our country can still admire 'typically Dutch' scenes of green meadows, canals, windmills and tulip fields. Yet it remains uncertain how much of it, in the long term, can be saved from urbanisation and economic pressure.

Now that you have (almost) finished reading this book, you should be ready for Dealing with the Dutch yourself. I'll conclude with summing up some of the advice given here, together with some hard facts about the country, its people, its economy and its history.

1. Noord means 'North'. As a result of long-past Belgian-Dutch political unity, *South-Brabant* is a Belgian province around Brussels. Confusingly, many Dutch people also simply refer to Noord-Brabant as 'Brabant'.
2. Recently the Ministry of the Environment and Urban planning suggested the term Delta Metropolis might be more appropriate.

Chapter 13

ON DO'S AND DON'TS

This list of some of the major Do's and Don'ts in the Dutch business world is a summation of the advice given in various chapters of this book and is intended as a handy everyday point of reference.

Do's and don'ts

When working / doing business with the Dutch:

• do come well-prepared, with detailed and practical information about your products, needs and capacities;

• do come to the heart of the matter quickly, within a few minutes at most;

• do try to present yourself as punctual, modest and practical;

• do try to give a positive, but realistic and not 'overdone', presentation of yourself, your product and your company;

• do concentrate seriously on the matter in hand, making only occasional small-talk or jokes, until the business itself is over and done with;

• do state your opinions clearly but unemotionally;

• do consult Dutch colleagues at all levels (but don't take up too much of their time!);

• do be prepared for criticism and learn to deal with it calmly;

• do be critical and outspoken about the Dutch too – they expect it and appreciate it;

• do be open to compromise during any form of negotiation;

• do keep the rational and emotional sides of your character separate during working hours;

• do take initiatives and don't be afraid of losing face by being creative or by asking questions;

• do bring up alternatives when something is said to be impossible;

• do ask Dutch colleagues their opinion on your performance (but be prepared for very honest answers!);

• do tell Dutch colleagues your views on their working environment and ways of doing things: 'constructive criticism' will be appreciated;

- do participate in company rituals such as colleagues' birthday coffee and cake, the 'borrel', Christmas celebrations, etc.;
- do try to learn to speak Dutch (and practise it!), even when the Dutch speak English to you;
- do read about – and ask questions about – Dutch history and society; this will help you to understand the Dutch better;
- do try, by your behaviour, to disprove any negative stereotypes of your country and fellow countrymen; and conversely, do try to avoid generalising about, and stereotyping, the Dutch.

- don't offer (or expect to be offered) expensive business gifts;
- don't, during the introduction, boast about academic degrees, influential family members or relationships with important people;
- don't overdress; see what other people are wearing and ask Dutch colleagues for advice;
- don't ask questions about the other person's income, political views or private life;
- don't expect lavish meals or sightseeing tours. But if you are offered them, it is obviously a good sign;
- don't, as an in-company visitor to Dutch headquarters, expect to be booked into the best hotel in town;
- don't expect intensive personal coaching by the host company outside working hours;
- don't expect the Dutch to come for a drink after work, but <u>do</u> continue to ask: one day they will come;
- don't, when selling, forget to mention any price and environmental advantages of your product;
- don't expect (and certainly don't ask for) any personal favours outside the transaction;
- don't shower the Dutch with compliments; it makes them uneasy;
- don't begin long discussions on philosophy, literature, art etc. during introductions, business lunches and in working hours;
- don't, when working with Dutch people, be 'bossy' to your subordinates, ask them for their opinion, and after some time show interest in their personal backgrounds.

Appendix

THE NETHERLANDS:
FACTS AND FIGURES

General The Netherlands lies in northwestern Europe. Germany is to the east and Belgium to the south. Across the North Sea, to the west, is Great Britain. The Netherlands is a small country – it is only 120 km from the beach at The Hague to the nearest German territory, and the maximum distance from north to south is a mere 400 km. The total area is 41,865 km² (15,770 sq. miles), including the Waddenzee and IJsselmeer. The land area is 33,800 km².

Climate The temperate maritime climate has winters with day temperatures around freezing point, often with strong winds. Snow and severe frost occur in rare severe winters. Summers can be hot and sunny (30+°C in the daytime, 20°C at night), but may also be disappointing, with much cooler, cloudy weather. Rain and humidity can occur in all seasons, which may make winter days very chilly and summer days sticky. The Dutch weather is changeable and unpredictable, which might explain its importance as a topic of casual conversation.

Scenery The country is flat, with much man-made land (reclaimed lakes and swamps) below sea level. This is generally true for the western part of the country, where water is to be seen almost everywhere: rivers, canals, lakes, estuaries and the omnipresent ditches that drain the low grasslands, giving them a neatly carved-up appearance. The lowest point, near Rotterdam, is some 7 meters (23 feet) below sea level.

The east and south of the country are slightly higher and drier. There you can find sandy elevations, areas of forest and heather, and in some places 'hills' some 100 meters in height. The highest point of the Netherlands (321 metres, 1053 feet.) is in the extreme southeast, in the province of Limburg.

Although the country is densely populated, strict building controls safeguard open spaces. The Netherlands has areas of outstanding natural beauty which are extremely popular with natives and visitors alike.

Natural resources   The main assets of the Dutch economy have always been its fertile soils and its favourable location on the rivers and seas of western Europe, which has stimulated trade for centuries. The Netherlands was always regarded as being quite poor in natural mineral resources. Up until the 1970s coal was produced in quantities that did not allow export, there was small-scale exploitation of oil and iron ore, and of clay and gravel for construction. But in 1960, enormous quantities of natural gas, and further quantities of oil, were discovered in the north of the country and in the Dutch coastal waters of the North Sea.

Economy   Probably because large areas of the country are flat and green, the Netherlands has a strongly agricultural image abroad. However, milk, cheese and flower bulbs by no means represent a realistic picture of the country. The agro-industry is much more varied than that, and the value of agricultural exports is second only to that of the USA. Just over 2% of all working people are employed in agriculture itself, a reflection of the high level of mechanisation and automation.

The Dutch economy is predominantly industrially and service-oriented, with a strongly international orientation based on the country's long trading tradition and colonial past. This is reflected in the disproportionately high number of multinational companies. Companies such as Ahold, Akzo-Nobel, DSM, Heineken, KLM, Philips, Shell, Stork, Unilever, Wolters-Kluwer/Reed-Elsevier, and financial organisations such as ABN/Amro, Aegon, ING, KPN and Rabobank are well-known abroad, but not always identified as being completely or partially Dutch.

The oil industry, machinery, electronics and other high-tech production, the large and varied agro-industry, together with transport and other trade-related facilities such as banking and insurance, are responsible for the bulk of the economic output.

The carefully managed exploitation and export of Holland's large reserves of natural gas has given the Dutch economy a sound basis since the early 1960s and is one reason why the guilder has become one of the world's strongest currencies.

Activities such as flower growing and the breeding of oysters and mussels for foreign markets are high-profile but, in fact, marginal when compared to the extent of more conventional activities. Few people realise that the banknotes of a large number of countries are printed in the Netherlands, that their CDs may have been produced here, their booming ports rebuilt, expanded or modernised by specialised Dutch building companies, their ships-in-trouble saved or salvaged by Dutch maritime services. They may enjoy Dutch beer or ice cream, cook with Dutch dried spices and, indeed, feed their babies on Dutch milk powder and, when they are older, treat them to Dutch candy. And they may have Dutch flowers in their vases and Dutch-printed posters on their walls.

On a more abstract – and culture-related – level, the Dutch economy can still be described as a mixture of free market economy and fairly strong government control, although the latter is decreasing. A deeply felt need to have everyone share a decent standard of living has led to a system in which, more than in most countries, the national wealth is distributed to all.

Another aspect of state control are the rules and regulations imposed on enterprises of all types. These concern matters such as safety and hygiene, salary levels, workers' rights, protection of the environment, limitations on building, and many, many others.

Yet Holland has much to offer to foreign investors: a highly educated work force; an excellent coastal position at the heart of the world's largest trading block, nearby emerging markets; a very good infrastructure; and, in spite of the otherwise high taxation, favourable tax rates for foreign investment.

Spread of population   With 16 million inhabitants the Netherlands is the world's fourth most densely populated country (after Bangladesh, Taiwan and South Korea). The spread of the population, and therefore of economic activity, is very uneven. The less populated areas are to be found in the northeast and the southwest. Nearly half the population lives in the west, in the so-called Randstad.

Language   Dutch, a Germanic language like German and English, is spoken throughout the country although there are various regional dialects. The province of Friesland, in the north, has its own language, related to Dutch.

Religion   From the 1500s onwards Calvinism, a rather strict Protestant denomination, dominated the region north of the three major rivers which cut through the middle of the country, while in the south the great majority remained Catholic. After World War II church going quickly declined. Nowadays, only some 25% of the Dutch regularly attend church services. Among the ethnic minorities Islam is the most widespread religion.

Education   Education in the Netherlands, organised in the continental European tradition, is good according to international standards, albeit with little mixture of theory and practice. Both state and private schools are government-funded and therefore free, or largely free, up to the age of 16. An extensive state scholarship system helps people over 16 to partially finance further studies, regardless of parental income.

State control has resulted in fairly even quality throughout the country, including the universities, although some faculties may enjoy a particularly good reputation. For jobs in the business world, MBA studies and HEAO (a sub-academic vocational training) are widely popular nowadays.

School attendance is obligatory up to the age of 16, but a substantial percentage of students continue into higher education. Some 7% of the population has completed an academic education.

For the children of people from overseas there are some schools with a British, American, German or Japanese curriculum.

Basic history

40 BC - 4th century AD Areas south of the river Rhine are part of the Roman Empire. To the north are tribal areas.

5th - 8th century The southern part of the Netherlands is part of the Frankish, Merovingian and Carolingian empires. The North is 'Free Frisian' territory.

8th - 10th century Charlemagne conquers the Frisians; from 870 on the Low Countries (including Belgium and Luxembourg) form part of the East Frankish Empire and, from 962, of the Holy Roman Empire.

11th - 14th century Feudalism was the dominant system in the higher-lying eastern areas. As the population grows, low-lying marshlands in the west come under cultivation. Peasants and fishermen build dykes to protect their property and lives, creating *waterschappen*, organisations for the construction, maintenance and repair of dykes and sluices. Many of the Dutch provinces were first established during these centuries. By the 1400s Hanseatic cities develop (maritime) trade with European countries.

15th and 16th century By inheritance, the Low Countries become part of the Burgundian empire, later they are ruled by Habsburg Spain. Hanseatic cities develop maritime trade with other European countries.

16th century Reformation gains many followers in the Low Countries. Reacting to oppression by Catholic Spain, the Protestants rise up and declare independence in 1581: the Republic of the Seven United Netherlands, a federation of the northern provinces led by the province of Holland. The Princes of Orange-Nassau are in power but are not regarded as royal. Calvinist religion comes to dominate. By around 1590 the rebellion has been won, but formally continues until 1648. The south remains Catholic, partly occupied by the Dutch republic, partly still under Spanish domination (this area was later to become Belgium).

17th century Pursuing the Spanish enemy and its ally Portugal, the Dutch republic develops a highly successful and worldwide maritime trade empire, ranging from the Baltic to focusing on the East Indian Archipelago, present day Indonesia. The Republic enters its Golden Age. Many prosper, cities expand, art flourishes, vast areas of land are reclaimed and the Republic acquires widespread international prestige. A national identity gradually develops.

18th century Stagnation of Dutch maritime trade in the face of British competition.

1795 - 1813 Anti-Orangist regime based on French revolutionary principles, followed by French occupation. Napoleon's brother Louis becomes the first king of this vassal state (1806). Catholicism once again becomes accepted.

1813 Restoration of independence, reunification with Belgium. The Prince of Orange becomes King. Belgium industrialises, the north remains mostly agrarian. North-south antagonisms increase. The word 'Netherlands' is used more often. Belgium secedes in 1830.

1880 After a period of stagnation, the country begins to industrialise and modernise. In Indonesia colonial rule and exploitation are intensified, bringing the Netherlands great profit. Various religious and political groups set up their own political parties, organisations and education systems, leading to social compartmentalisation.

1914 - 1918 The Netherlands remains neutral in World War I. The 1916 floods lead to the closing off and reclaiming of the Zuiderzee in decades to follow.

1920s Modest prosperity, increasing industrialisation and modernisation. Radio is introduced, organised into separate socio-religious broadcasting organisations.

1930s Severe economic crisis, the government increases its grip on the economy in an attempt to solve massive unemployment .

1940 - 1945 Nazi occupation, 100,000 Dutch Jews perish in concentration camps, another 100,000 people in acts of war and other acts of repression. Enormous economic problems ensue. From 1941 on, Japan occupies the Dutch East Indies. In the face of the German occupation, social compartmentalisation is temporarily overcome.

1945 – 1950 Liberation by the Allied armies. After Japan's occupation of the Dutch East Indies, the colony declares independence. For 4 years Dutch forces unsuccessfully fight against this. Colonial functionaries and the military, including many of its own citizens, are expelled by newly-independent Indonesia.

1950s With US aid ('Marshall-aid'), the Netherlands slowly recovers its prosperity. Hard work, thrift and acquiescence to leadership are emphasised. The 1953 flooding in the southwest (1850 people die), results in the Delta project, linking the islands and closing out the sea.

1960s The beginning of the welfare state, partly made possible by the discovery and exploitation of large quantities of natural gas. Student protests against the authoritarian education system lead to a youth revolt and vast social changes after 1965. This results in more democratic relationships and the loosening of religious bonds. Gradually, the old-style system of social compartmentalisation starts to dissolve.

1970s More prosperous than ever before. Under strong social-democratic influence, social benefits and taxes grow to the highest levels in the world. Labour immigration from Turkey and Morocco, and people from former Caribbean colonies create ethnic minorities.

1980s Under liberal/Christian-democratic government the country is faced with economic recession, growing unemployment and persistent state budget deficits. There are attempts at cutting back on welfare and other state expenditure. The 1982 agreement between trade unions and employers lays the foundation of the later 'economic miracle'. Some ethnic tensions begin to emerge in the cities.

1990s The economic recovery finally leads to an unprecedented prosperity. After 1994, consecutive liberal/ social-democratic governments stimulate self-employment and further 'deregulation'. This leads to the creation of many jobs and to economic growth higher than in surrounding countries: the 'Dutch economic miracle' or the 'polder model'.

With continuous immigration, the 'ethnic' groups grow to over 10% of the total population.

Large infrastructural works are under way: the Rotterdam-Germany freight railway line, high speed trains, the further expansion of Schiphol airport.

2000 At the beginning of the new millennium the Dutch economy continues to prosper and prospects remain good.

INDEX

Bold indicates a main section on the subject